The
WIDOW'S MIGHT

Jan Thompson

THE
WIDOW'S MIGHT

THE STRENGTH TO BE A VICTORIOUS SURVIVOR

JAN THOMPSON

TATE PUBLISHING & *Enterprises*

TATE PUBLISHING
& Enterprises

Tate Publishing is committed to excellence in the publishing industry. Our staff of highly trained professionals, including editors, graphic designers, and marketing personnel, work together to produce the very finest books available. The company reflects the philosophy established by the founders, based on Psalms 68:11,

"THE LORD GAVE THE WORD AND GREAT WAS THE COMPANY OF THOSE WHO PUBLISHED IT."

If you would like further information, please contact us:
1.888.361.9473 | www.tatepublishing.com
TATE PUBLISHING & Enterprises, LLC | 127 E. Trade Center Terrace
Mustang, Oklahoma 73064 USA

Cover design by Lynly Taylor
Interior design by Elizabeth Mason

Published in the United States of America

ISBN: 1–6024706–3-4
01.02.07

I dedicate this book to the memory of Lee Wesley Reuck and to the glory of God. It is written in the hope that for all those women who walk away from the grave of their beloved, it will provide an encouragement and a reminder that they are not the first, or the last, to experience the feelings they don't know what to do with.

ACKNOWLEDGEMENTS

Six weeks after I became a widow, two widows in their early thirties invited me to dinner. They told me their stories and patiently listened as I attempted telling mine through tears of despair. We had never met, but one woman was a friend of my daughter and insisted on taking time to minister to me. She brought a friend with her and they shared the tragic events of their husbands' accidental deaths. My heart ached for these women and their young children.

Before the evening was over, I had grown to love these women and developed a profound desire to pass their ministry on as well. To Christy Tucker and Karen Shelton, I shall ever be grateful for the beauty of that night. I have thought of them many times on my journey and kept them ever in my prayers. They exemplified "The Widow's Might" before I knew it existed.

Thank you, Rindi Broussard, for holding my hand all night long that last night and many times after; Betty and Ed Miller, for your patience and generosity that went many extra miles, and Brother Rick Cundieff for making Lee's service an inspiration and comfort to everyone present. People still remark of the beauty that it was. Thank you, Helen Anne Bruner, for being my best friend, no matter what happens, ever; and to my children, Jamie and Glen Dunnam and Julie Harris, for being a source of strength and hope.

And finally, thank you, Jim Thompson, for encouraging me to share the widow's might with others. I am blessed beyond measure.

Table of Contents

Introduction

In the first moments following the death of my husband I remember thinking over and over again, "What am I going to do? What do I do now?"

The days turned into weeks and the weeks into months, and until the end of the seventh month, I was a real mess. I cried every single day, and sometimes I would weep uncontrollably all day long. The finality of it all was more than my heart could absorb or my mind would acknowledge. I kept expecting him to come through the door or call. But, of course, he didn't, and I was left to figure out how to deal with being alone.

There were so many who tried to minister to me, but they didn't know what to say or do. How could they? They could not know my pain. They were not married to the wonderful man who had filled my life so beautifully every day for all those years. It seemed that every time I turned around, others handed me new books on how to grieve. What were they thinking? I *knew* how to grieve! Someone needed to show me how to heal. Do that and you have something.

There were times when I cried so hard that I could hardly get my breath and times when all I wanted to do was scream to the world, "Don't you know my husband is dead? How dare you laugh, tell jokes, and proceed with your lives as though nothing has happened." But the world still spins and I inhaled and exhaled, and the days passed, and I found out how long the nights really are.

From time to time I would encounter another widow and we would compare "war stories", and just the sharing of them eased the pain for a moment. I found that I was not the only one having these thoughts and feelings, and the sharing helped remove the guilt for having them.

I discovered very early that it was very therapeutic to inform others that my husband had recently died. I am not sure why I felt compelled to tell people, for I genuinely did not seek any kind of pity, but it seemed to help me better accept the fact of it all. When I said it, I heard it, my psyche acknowledged it, and my mind got used to hearing the truth. I met other women who had experienced the deaths of their mates, and we bonded for a moment. Some had remarried. Some had never healed. Others had done very well; and some said, "It doesn't get any easier," while others assured me that it did get easier with the passage of time. My conclusion was that, indeed, we are all very different with different ways of dealing with our pain. And my heart broke for those who did not seem to have healed even one bit in the time that had passed since the deaths that had stopped their own lives as well.

I wanted to reassure myself and others that God still has a purpose for us here, and we must be about seeking and fulfilling it. I wanted hope for the morrow and the firm belief that joy could be experienced again.

While perusing a catalog that came in the mail one day, I noticed a pewter heart pin. The heart had a crack down the middle of it and a Band-Aid taped across it. It screamed at me, "This is you, Jan. You have a broken heart, but you are mending. You are healing." I called immediately and ordered five of the hearts. I had been ministered to by two young widows shortly after Lee died. I met a widow whose husband died of brain cancer three weeks after Lee. And I wanted to order an extra should I encounter another such as I.

In the time between the call ordering the five mending hearts, the Lord gave me a vision. It just all came together so beautifully that I could hardly believe how well it seemed to fit. I saw a book reaching out to widows who, like me, wanted something to hold onto. The Bible is the most perfect and obvious choice, but I wanted *"first-hand, down and dirty how I survived"* dialogue and the story of the widow's mite came to my mind. Then I thought, "Lord, I need might to get me through this, and I know you can empower me to do this thing and anything else you want of me." I imagined support conferences for widows with financial and career planning, makeovers, counseling, and a new start in this thing called widowhood. Women could come together for a weekend to share their losses with other widows and find a new direction for their lives. The word *widow* has a negative connotation to it; I wanted to take the negative, develop it and see a new and beautiful picture.

I don't have any sage advice; I just present to grieving widows what I have experienced and the conclusions the Lord has placed on my heart. We need the support of one another; the reassurance that we are going to make it through the maze of this pain. That is my desire for each of us as we set out to honor the precious memory of our dear husbands; to live the rest of our lives in grace and dignity, and, in all we do, to glorify the Father. If we can do those things, we are well on our way to healing and having a true victory over the grave.

May God bless you as you seek answers. If you find them, share them. If you do not, move on to the next question, because there will be many more. The final answer to any of your questions is that God loves you and even though you don't understand what He is doing, trust Him; just trust Him. You will be given strength you never dreamed of. But depend on the Almighty, and you *will* have might, *The Widow's Might,* to meet the challenges and joys of a life God wants to use. Please let me know how you get on. I truly care how you shall handle this detour.

The Widow's Mite

"And Jesus sat over against the treasury, and beheld how the people cast money into the treasury; and many that were rich cast in much.

And there came a certain poor widow, and she threw in two mites, which make a farthing.

And he called unto him his disciples, and saith unto them, "Verily I say unto you, that this poor widow hath cast more in, than all they which have cast into the treasury:

For all they did cast in of their abundance; but she of her want did cast in all that she had, even all her living."

Mark 12: 41–44

MITE TO MIGHT

Jesus tells of the widow who threw two mites into the treasury in the presence of those who cast in much and declares to his disciples that she had cast in more than all the others. The widow not only gave, but gave all she had. Now that I am a widow myself, I think of this story and determine that I, too, shall cast into the treasury my mite. But I think of another might as well and ask from where will the power and strength to live come? It will be a might given to me from God to empower me in daily tasks and trials. Where will I acquire the strength to go on without my mate? How will I provide for my needs, not just financially, but in every aspect of my life? I must plug myself into the mighty source of God who will empower me to overcome the world with all He expects of me and puts in place for me. He has given me the strength to be about His will for my life. This strength is not only to sustain me but also to go forward and touch the world with sensitivity and beauty.

It has been said that a seed has to die, be buried and let time pass, and then it emerges into newness. This is how it is to be with the widow. Death must not stop us. It can fertilize us, even prune us, but it must not stop us. We carry within our tender hearts the widow's might. We will not waste such a thing, but we will use it to the glory of our Lord and the preservation of our very sanity. Our contribution can be great if we but cast it in.

"I am weary with my groaning: all the night make I my bed to swim; I water my couch with my tears." Psalm 6:6

A Degree

One morning I placed my husband's head in my lap, stroked his beautiful salt and pepper gray hair, and released him into the arms of God. When the funeral directors came to take his body, I placed rose petals upon the gurney where they would lay him and take him forever from our home. It was a sobering thing to observe. As they drove down our gravel driveway, I walked into our field of bluebonnets, which my husband had so loved, and watched the vehicle quietly drive out of sight. The bluebonnets were also preparing for their own deaths as they faded and used their last energy to seed for another season of blooming.

In the weeks since that morning, I have been forced to attend a university of sorts. The course is Widowhood and before even the first class, "101", I was required to attend orientation. The trip to the funeral home, selecting his clothes for the service, picking out a casket, going to the cemetery to select the place where they would bury him, was just the first part of orientation. I then needed to select the music, a speaker, and help with the content of his service. If there was some way to video the widow in her first few hours and days into this sorority, one would observe the strength of a gladiator. She is required to do, under unbelievable stress, things that do not seem real, because they are so painful. This is where shock becomes a friend. We go through the motions in a bubble. It can last for months.

When the shock drops you hard on your bippy, you drag yourself to class; Widowhood 101. Here is where you send off death certificates and inform social security, banks, attorneys and creditors what has happened. You get a date; a date to go to court to probate his will. You must prove to the world that he loved you enough to remember you in this final way. You must prove that you are entitled to what is yours already. Everything is quite clinical and the legal jargon can be upsetting. The judge will ask you if you were indeed married to the man whose will is before him. (Why on God's earth would I be here otherwise?) After identification of each of us is established and the question of minor children is answered, a few other legal issues are addressed, signatures are applied to documents and it is done.

Then Widowhood: Reality Check is your next course of study. Your married friends must think your condition is contagious because the invitations to dinner and fellowship end. The same Friday and Saturday nights that used to be special and celebratory are now empty. Things that come in two's seem superfluous and cruel now. You wonder if you should consider a twin bed because the queen bed has lost its king. Reality check is deciding what to do with his clothes, his jewelry, toothbrush, shoes, briefcase, and wallet. How can things that once were so important and necessary be so worthless now? Do I just throw out his contact lens? Yes, I know that I should donate them to someone, some place, but I don't want to make the calls.

Then we move on to Widowhood: the Nothingness. This is the course where you wonder why you bother taking a bath or washing your hair. You go through the motions of changing sheets every week because you always did, but why? You haven't slept on them anyway. You take care of necessities like paying the electric bill, buying dog food, and opening your mail. Dear God, when will all those sympathy cards stop? I know they mean well, but their kindness is just too tender right now. Every single time I open another one I start crying all over again.

The reason for any of it escapes you and you just go through the motions of the nothingness. The china has lost its luster, the goblets could as easily be jelly glasses and the gourmet cook is eating peanut butter from a jar. You didn't lose your husband; you lost yourself. You know exactly where he is, but where are you?

Then one day, Widowhood, the Bottom is the course you must travail. This is the one where your sex drive comes back and there is nothing to do about it. This is where you are reminded how very alone you really are. You ache for the touch of a human hand; someone to hold you and tell you everything will be okay. This is where you cannot believe how a heart can hurt and still function. You remember just enough for it to mock you how a kiss on the neck can thrill you. Hugging a pillow or a cat is an empty exercise. A vibrator is not a lover. You want to be loved with all you are made of and you want to love something besides a memory; something alive. A memory cannot gaze into your eyes across the table; it will not tell you how pretty you look tonight. "Widowhood, the Bottom" is a very difficult course in your education. You get a passing grade if you just survive it.

If you are still standing for your next class, take heed, it might be what casts you down; "Recovery, Re-entry;" back to the business of relationships. Step slowly and softly here, and the most important thing you can do is to be true to your Lord and yourself; in doing that, you will side-step regrets later on. Be honest with yourself and others. Don't pretend to be further along than you really are. In every moment seek to be the best person you know how to be. Don't make unrealistic demands of yourself or others.

God is preparing a new life for you in direct parallel to your needs and desires. You will earn your Masters degree in widowhood *from* the Master. I pray you use your education well. I pray that you become stronger through the course. If you are still standing after this course, you are stronger.

I shall see you at the commencement exercises. Remember that commencement means *beginning*. I display my degree proudly; my instructor was God and my husband paid for the course. I must use it well.

I Was Left Behind

I have enjoyed the phenomenally popular book series known as *Left Behind* by Tim LaHaye and Jerry B. Jenkins. It is the story of the Rapture taking place and those people who were not Christians left here on earth to survive without the presence of their loved ones who have gone on to be with the Lord.

Although I have not missed the Rapture and am confident that when that happens, I will not be left behind, my beloved has gone on without me to a higher plane. While I am pleased that he is no longer sick or sore, I miss him more than I can possibly describe. The pain of his absence is one for which no painkiller has ever been manufactured. And just when I thought I could not bear the pain another moment, numbness arrived and saturated my spirit.

I have been an enthusiastic, high spirited optimist for much of my life. Having loved and been loved by my wonderful husband gave me reason for such demeanor. Yet, in the days and months since he left my life, the void of his smile has snuffed most of the light from my world. How can I ever see clearly again, and what is there to see? Of course, I know that the power source in my life is the Lord and He does not intend my living in darkness. Maybe at some given time He will put another light in my life; I really don't know.

I *do* know that it is not fun being left behind. It is like a terrible nightmare in a book of fiction. It is the same in the non-fiction I live every day. I don't eat right, exercise properly, or care much about my appearance. My only nutrition is hope; the hope that I shall find something to look forward to again; something that tastes good again, and some exercise that will make sense. I live on hope.

Not only do I feel left behind, but I feel left out. Is the whole world "coupled-off", or does it just appear that way to those of us who are alone? Chris Carlson is the talented designer of the beautifully decorated women's wear line, "Christine Alexander". She is also my friend who sent me a most sensitive and wonderful card after my husband died. It showed a cat, a dog and a squirrel looking out a window at a critter walking into the distant sunset. When I opened the card, it said simply, "He isn't gone, he's just gone ahead." It was a comfort to me because as I looked around my world, it definitely appeared that he was gone. Thinking of him as just having gone ahead of me to that future destination was a sweet thought. I regret that I don't know the name of the artist or card company who produced the card, but it touched me deeply and profoundly.

Yes, I am left behind, but at some point, we shall all arrive at that place together. I believe I was left because there is a task or purpose I must attend. Being left behind in this context is not punishment, but a challenge and an opportunity. I shall use what is left; of me, of my resources, of my very soul to live again.

A PRAYER

Dear God:

My beautiful husband is dead, but You know that, don't You. Only You tell me that he isn't dead; but that he lives more beautifully even than before; and that his body is healed. My fellow Christians tell me this too as though it will be a comfort. Well, my loving Father, why do they only have patronizing answers? Show me someone who can tell me why he had to be sick in the first place. We tried so hard to do the right things; eat right, exercise, serve you, read and listen to uplifting material and music, adore each other, and glory in You. While those around us wasted themselves in trash food, alcohol, tobacco, infidelity, no joy in life or in You; we tried to beacon You. His holy temple (his body), deteriorated even though we tried to honor it. And God! All Your wonderful words I committed to memory so I could remind myself every moment that we could "move this mountain (of cancer), and cast it into the sea." *[1] How could I interpret them so badly? We took heart and courage in believing that Your love, Your protection, and promises would heal him. But heal him *here.* I confess I am selfish. I want him here with me now, to touch, feed, laugh with, sleep with, work and play with.

Eternity is so long. What was Your hurry? Oh God! I loved him so. We were truly one. What am I now without him? Half; half of what?

My friends feel compelled to comfort me with words so familiar that I know what they are going to say before they speak them. They are of no comfort. Please forgive me if I offend, but right now even Your words are little comfort.

My only comfort is that I know You, and I know You love me, and in that love You do what is best for me; and that You have this great big plan for my life. I do not have to (or even get to) understand what You are doing. I must trust only You, and I do. That trust doesn't mean I don't ache with the pain of my husband's new life without me, but I do know that when I see him again, I'll understand. For now, I truly do "see through a glass darkly." *2

Since my beloved mate is not here to provide for and protect me, I now depend completely on You for that. After all, it was really You that did it through my husband anyway. Now what will you use? God, I ask for wisdom, courage, discernment, sharp instincts to develop and grow into what is next. I ask for the right people, ideas, and talents for the molding of my life that You are forming.

Make me strong; I know there will be pain. May the memories and joys we have made and known hold me up instead of throwing me to my knees. For all the things we had and were together must mean more than just the moments we lived them. They were building blocks for what is next, and they will stand well, for they are on the foundation of Your love and grace.

Help me make the rest of my life one that all Heaven will smile upon, and one that will make both You and my husband proud.

"I can do all things through Christ which strengtheneth me." Philippians 4:13

Amen
*1 *Mark 11:23–24*
*2 *I Corinthians 13:12*

Two Weeks and Five Days

I want to forget; at least for a few moments so that my *griever* can rest. I want to remember how to laugh; I cannot think of how it is done. I want to feel pretty again; he made me feel pretty. I want to care about something; anything; I don't. I am so empty, and so useless. Oh God! Oh God! Oh dear God!

LIFE'S SONG

It has occurred to me that each one of us is a song. Each song is unique with its own melody and distinct verses. There are many verses to each song, as it tells the story of each life.

The first verse is our birth and childhood. The second can be young adulthood or early marriage. The following verses tell a story of bearing children, building a house, teenagers, perhaps a career, children off to college, empty nest, special times spent with your spouse throughout your song. You may make plans for new verses you want to write, but sometimes a verse gets written for you; a verse you never expected or at least for a long time to come. When your spouse dies, and that is written into the ballad of your life, you want your song to just end, for it has taken a sour note. The rhythm is out of sync, and there seems to be no rhyme or reason.

You may wish for your song to end, but it continues somehow. You wonder what the next verse could possibly be and are afraid to even try writing it. Your song becomes a low hum. But through it all, you must know that your song has a chorus and that although the verses tell of what happens to you, your chorus is the theme of your life. Your chorus is who you always were; the chorus that is familiar, no matter what happens. It might help to take a pen and write down the words to your chorus as you hear it from within.

Until you begin to write new verses, hum your chorus, sing it, dance to it. Your song is beautiful and others long to hear it. Sing your song. Sing your life. The verses will come. The master conductor is on His stand, and He is ready to make your life a beautiful symphony. And those who will bring harmony to your song will bless you more than you can imagine.

"Sing unto him a new song; play skillfully with a loud noise." Psalm 33:3

Preparation for Widowhood

Someone asked me if I had any advice for preparing for widowhood. Of course there are the things one should do regardless of circumstance. One should have a current will in a secure place, knowledge of the financial and insurance information pertinent to the household and banking matters; and the most important thing in any situation is the assurance that your husband knows the Savior. He must be truly prepared to meet his creator, having known and accepted Jesus Christ.

Apart from these things which are of great import in every family, with or without threat of the grave, I would say there can be no real preparation for such an event. One cannot know the agony this side of the grave until that day. Even if there has been a long and painful illness where death seems the kindest answer for everyone involved, the finality of the grave is so overwhelming that it cannot be imagined before its arrival. Therefore, I believe we should prepare to meet each day with all the love we can and make it beautifully evident to him with each breath he and you share. These precious moments of care that you are privileged to administer are gifts to you and from you that only Heaven can measure. As much as possible, stay close to him, read to him, touch him often, play music he loves, talk to him sweetly, and even feed him as much as is possible what he loves most. And when you are called upon to do things you never imagined you would need to do for your lover and mate, consider it a high honor that you are available and capable of doing them. Help him maintain his dignity as you approach each task with thankfulness in your heart that it is you instead of some stranger who is there caring for him. If you are called upon to swab his mouth, kiss it first. If his mustache needs trimming, remind him how handsome he still is, and if any bodily function does not perform as expected, give high praises to God that it is you who can be there to right it for him. This is the man you pledged to love in sickness and in health till death separates you. These days, months or years can be a final expression and dimension of love you could not have imagined if not for this condition.

Of course your own health and psyche must be tended and there will be times when you despair, but there will be plenty of time for that when Heaven bids him home. For now, get your house in order; ask questions if he is able to communicate. But even if he is incapable of communicating with you, you have no idea of what he is aware. See that everything he hears is bathed in love and prayer; let no one utter negative statements or grim dialogue in his presence. Remind him with every touch and glance that he is your beloved. When he sleeps; rest. If hospice comes to bathe him so that you can tend your own hygiene, take advantage of it with a thankful heart. Do all you can to cherish these moments he holds onto the life that the two of you have shared.

When you walk away from the cemetery at that assigned time, you will walk away knowing that you did all you could to bring about cure, comfort and class to that grand assignment to which you were privileged to perform. We must attempt in all areas of our life to manage whatever our tasks at hand with dignity, grace and gratitude. God will not require more of us than we are capable of handling. That does not mean He will not require of us more than we desire or want to deal with. And it does not mean we even know how to do what will be required or expected of us. We don't have to worry that we don't know how to do this thing. When He requires of you a new route, a detour you don't want to take, He will provide the guidance and grace to take it.

How to prepare for the position of widowhood? Be the best wife you can possibly be; gentle, loving, tender-hearted, sweet-spirited so that you will be able to look back with pride at how you accepted the challenges of the time. There is nothing as final as death. The day will come when you can no longer touch his precious face, kiss his brow, or turn him over in bed. The day will come when you throw out the feeding tubes, the Pampers, and the medicine forever. While he yet breathes and has a blood pressure to measure, love him with all you are. Perhaps when the title of widow is cast upon you, there will be no regret for what you might have done. There will be plenty of things you will be called upon to address, try to forgo that of regret.

Bridge of Faith

I have been on this road for some while now and I have come upon a place in the road where I must make a decision. The road has come to an abrupt end whereupon there are choices to be made. To the left is a place called "Understanding". To the right is the road to "Confusion," and straight ahead is a bridge that ascends high into the sky. I can see that the bridge is named "Bridge of Faith."

I stand at the end of this "Sorrow Road" knowing I have choices to make. The obvious choice is just to stay where I am and grieve and mourn for all the pain and heartache I have experienced. I can stay here for as long as I desire. I can even turn around and walk the road again and again, basking in the sorrow that I have found along the way. It is tempting.

I look to the left at the place called "Understanding" and I can see so many things I love and relate to. I see little girls playing happily together, and from time to time they run to their mother with glee and hug her neck and place a wreath of flowers upon her head. I see a husband whispering love secrets to his wife with his hand wrapped around hers as they stroll along the shoreline. I see puppies and kittens and flowers and little yellow houses with white picket fences around. There are magnolia trees blooming with the sweet aroma of citrus. There are church steeples; and smiles are abundant there. I have lived in this very place and attempt to return. But I cannot find the entrance anymore. There is a "detour" sign pointing to "Faith Bridge" but I am not ready to go there. I want to return to "Understanding" and familiar surroundings. But alas, there is no way to get there. It is barricaded and a large "Road Closed" sign posted.

I look to the right and see the sign that reads, "Confusion - Just Ahead." I do not desire to go to any state of confusion but think maybe it might wind around and I can find my way to Understanding again. Maybe a new road is being built beyond Confusion. So I strike out and immediately notice cemeteries with new graves and weeping widows. I see blindness in old women and despair in old men. There is anger and bitterness here, but a thing even worse. There is numbness. It is worse than the pain I have come to know. I do not want to live in Confusion where the water is laced with a drug that constrains the mind, the heart, the very soul of those who dwell there. I must get back to Sorrow and decide what to do.

Here I am again at my sorrow. I return to it much too often. Shall I just pitch a little tent here and live out my days, and plant only memory seeds so that all I ever know is what I *have* known? No! That would truly be a sad thing and I do not, must not, add to the sorrows that already are licking at my feet.

I stand staring at the "Bridge of Faith" sign. I have no idea what is beyond. The uncertainty is frightening and the unknown is more than I can comprehend. Why would I take this bridge? If I could just get back to Understanding, but that road is closed to me now. I am told that there is a field on the other side of this bridge that is called "Freedom." It is a field free of the need to understand what has happened. It is freedom from despair. It is a field of new beauties, new opportunities, freshness, and scope that one can only experience by taking the bridge. I do not like having to make choices. But by not choosing one, I choose another. So here I go. I must hope the builder of this bridge knew what he was doing so that it will not collapse with the weight of my sorrow.

The first step was the most difficult but the bridge held sorrow's weight. I notice it seems to be constructed of old and rugged wood. There are bloodstains and there are holes that seem to have been made by large spikes. What kind of carpenter would build such a bridge?

As I climb higher upon this ascending bridge, I have a better view of things; and it is not so frightening being here after all. Maybe that is why they call it Faith; or is it because I was so afraid and I took the Bridge of Faith as my only way out of fear and despair. I conclude that it doesn't matter. I am beginning to experience a new sense of freedom and I am not even to that field yet. Where does freedom begin? I believe it began with that first step onto Faith Bridge. This could be very exciting; it could even be wonderful. Oh, thank you, Master Carpenter, who built this mighty structure over which I may conquer sorrow; where I no longer have the need for understanding and am not plagued with confusion. I am on my way to Freedom, and I know it cost you dearly.

Learning Before the Teacher Arrives

When my father-in-law died several years ago, I recall the look of desperation on the face of my husband's mother. She wrung her hands and fidgeted constantly. She walked around in circles and seemed lost. She cried when you looked at her, and when you didn't. We were advised of every detail for which she was now responsible regarding his death. I remember how when she spoke of his life before he died, it was, "Before he got sick," which translated to before he died. She would not use the word as if it might not be true if she didn't say it. We hugged her a lot but nothing really helped and so we avoided the subject as much as possible for lack of any knowledge of how to help her.

I wonder now, from my own perspective as a new widow, what I might have done to have helped her through the most difficult of times. After his father had been dead for one year, my husband told his mother often that she had cried long enough and she needed to get on with her life. I, too, bought into the theory that a year is surely enough time to get over such a thing and, after all, life is for the living. Get on with it.

My beloved husband is dead and I am still partially in shock from the realization of his death. I still find it very difficult to accept the reality of it and I find that I cry when people look at me, and frequently, when they don't. I have also noticed that I feel some need to inform my children of the little details of death certificates and legal matters regarding his death, and I, too, try to think of friendlier terms for what has happened than that totally final word, Death.

We thought my father-in-law's death happened to us as well as to her. I suppose in a way it did, for we loved him dearly. But comparing the pain of loss in the death of a father to the death of a life-mate is a study in futility. Who does she now ask opinions of, complain about taxes to, plan a garden with, eat with, make coffee for? It isn't the legal or financial details that come to mind when I think of how much I miss my husband; it is the lift of his eyebrow, or the wink of his eye across the room; it is the smell of him, the joy of folding his laundry, and marveling at his physical strength, and ten million other aspects of his beautiful life.

I wish I knew how to convey to my mother-in-law some sense of compassion for her pain and sorrow. I do not, but I want to learn. I want to touch her and somehow take on part of that terrible burden of pain. I want to help her carry it, or at least let her know that I now truly understand why she would wring her hands. What else do you do with hands that used to serve him? Where do you put them? It's like being on stage and not knowing what to do with them. They used to be employed in so many things on his behalf; now they just sign on a dotted line where he cannot.

Now I must make myself think of others more so than myself. My mother-in-law not only gave her husband up to death, but now her only child has been called home as well. I do not want to fail her this time in our shared agony. I did not wish to join this sorority of sorrow; membership was forced upon me. I now attempt doing my duty in this new calling. As I wring my hands and pace the floor in circles, I commit to a new level of compassion and empathy for my sisters-in-widowhood. Oh! To have become more sensitive to it all without having had to experience it first hand. We must learn more, faster, and better; hopefully before it is our turn.

An Empty Nest

Sometime in the night the barn swallow's nest on my front porch was destroyed. I suspect my cat. There were four babies in the nest, now gone. I do hope they were able to fly away. The nest was constructed of mud and has only a small section left. There is a huge gaping hole where life used to perch; much like *my* nest.

Six weeks ago cancer came to my nest and destroyed much of it as well. My baby, my beloved husband, is now gone; but alas, I know he was able to fly away. He sits upon a lofty perch where no harm will ever reach him again.

As the swallows keep returning and departing what is left of their home, they squeal and squawk in disbelief and panic. They hover and try in vain to capture what is no longer there.

I see myself in their desperation. I flail and squawk and hover in agony. But as summer follows spring, the swallows will build again their nest even in the face of danger and uncertainty, and so must I. So must we all.

These Things I Ask

Reveal to me, dear God, how I shall live the rest
of my life.
Tell it to my ear; speak it to my soul.
Place my feet upon that sacred path you have
cleared for me.
Canopy my life with your watch-care and elevate my
senses to new levels.
To my sight, add insight.
To my hearing; whisper the vibrating pulse of living
the moment.
To my touch, add the stroke of peace.
To my taste, give me a palate of discernment.
To my nostrils, breathe the fragrance of purpose.
Fill this gigantic hole with your tender mercies.
Remove the shackles from my spirit that I may not
be bound to pain or disillusionment.
Soar me, oh God, into a new joy.
Breathe into me hope for tomorrow, and
Keep me ever in Your palm.
(Forty days a widow)

What Can One Say?

As a widow of just over four months, I find myself in what can only be described as "between". I am no longer living in the joys I experienced with my husband and I have no idea what can possibly be next. This time last year my life was full of my husband, our plans, our dreams, our business. I go through the motions of commerce to keep the wolf away from the door, but zest and enthusiasm for it all has escaped me. I frequently tell myself that this is a temporary condition and is to be expected from one who has had her life-mate removed from her world. But, in truth, I wonder if I shall ever really emerge from this despair dungeon.

I know all the patronizing remarks. I have been guilty of expressing them to those who have preceded me on this journey. I am embarrassed at having to listen to those words, so well meaning, but so ignorant of any helpful wisdom, for they echo my own hollow attempts to ease the pain of some broken spirit.

What could others say to me right now to encourage or edify me? For one, they should not even presume to think they have a clue about how deeply I am hurting. They cannot go to this place, so they must not attempt telling me how to survive it, or even how to exit it. Even those who have been thrust into their own widowhood cannot fully know my agony for they did not know my absolute joy. How can they have any idea of my absolute agony? I am convinced that the more complete the joy and the deeper the love for the one who has gone ahead, the deeper the hole that is left within. It is my job to determine how to fill that hole.

I regret that I am so self-centered right now, for this is against my nature and I must not allow it to become engrained into the new person that I am becoming. It seems that I make almost everything that happens about me, and in reality, it just isn't. When I hear a song we loved, it is being played on my behalf, the minister's sermon speaks directly to me, and even the stars in the black night remind me he is not here to stand with me in awe of their wonder.

I do find it helpful when others simply remind me that they love me. And lately it has been of some assistance when I have been reminded that I am strong, although I don't feel it, and that God has some absolutely wonderful things in store for me, though I cannot imagine what, and with no advice at all, someone just says, "You are so special, and joy will once again fill you, in God's time." I guess it is like saying, "The sun will come out tomorrow," although, most of the time, I don't seem to care whether it does or not.

Of all the advances toward me, the tenderest thing anyone has done was to hug me and smile with an expression that spoke, "I don't know what to say about how you must be hurting, but I love you and am sorry to know that you are in such pain." I could have imagined that for my own benefit, but even if I did, that hug and gentle, loving smile was more healing than ten thousand words could have been.

It has been said, "With every good-bye you learn." I don't know what I have learned by having to say good-bye to that enchanted life with my husband. I just need it to have meant something positive, something beautiful.

Out of Focus

For years I have been a devoted fan of "Focus on the Family", a Christian radio program and outreach dedicated to encouraging and supporting Bible based values in relationship to the family. Dr. James Dobson does a wonderful job educating and ministering on behalf of the family and I have related to countless subjects that have been handled with sensitivity and grace. I have passed on my appreciation to my two daughters who also are charmed and warmed by the programming. But I became a widow five months ago and suddenly I don't feel like a family anymore. My children have been wonderful and supportive to me, but I am missing somehow the connection that made me feel complete in the family unit. My husband was a quiet and loving man whose presence just made everything right. He wanted to go to bed long before anyone else was ready, which drove us all crazy, and he sometimes would just smile and observe the goings-on, but we all felt his presence in each moment. And at any given time he might surprise us all with a chorus or a jig. His spontaneity kept us all guessing what he might do next; he was a joy.

The holidays are quickly approaching, and my focus is not on my family, but on what is *not* anymore. What do I do about Thanksgiving, and for what will I express gratitude? Sure I know all the right things to say; our health, for all the precious memories, for what is left, and for what is next, blah, blah, blah. Whom am I kidding? I want to skip Thanksgiving, Christmas, New Years, and anything else we are supposed to celebrate. And then, of course, shortly after those holidays, we observe St. Valentines Day. When did holidays become so cruel? I don't feel like celebrating. Where are my lessons learned from Christian programming? Focus? Focus on what? I can hardly see through my tear-filled eyes. I realize my grandchildren miss him too and will need to draw near to me and have the assurance that their grandmother is doing all right. Life does truly go on, whether we are ready for it or not. Focus? Right now things are pretty much a blur, but I know that somewhere down deep where the Holy Spirit is rooted, that a new sprout is preparing to emerge.

I cannot focus very well right now. I cannot see anything clearly yet, but I know if I just look toward God that His hand is on the lens of my life and when He is ready for me to have a clear picture, I will. Now I feel blinded by what has happened; but if even in the blur, I follow His lead, feel His grip on me; that soon I shall be able to focus again. Focus on the Savior. That's all the view I need right now.

Psalm 32:8 tells us, "I will instruct thee and teach thee in the way which thou shall go. I will guide thee with mine eye."

Wow! To Be Guided With God's Vision. Focus on that!

Detour

Life has a way of delivering circumstances for which we never reckoned, never planned for, and never thought possible to survive. One of these circumstances is the death of a spouse. We know that at some given time *down the road* one spouse or the other will have to deal with death, but somehow we think it is reserved for those in their eighties or nineties.

The detour of death can really throw one off track. Detours are such inconveniences; no one likes taking them. They slow you down considerably and sometimes you can get lost on a route you've never taken before. The death of a spouse is much like this. It is an extreme inconvenience to say the least. After all, we had plans! Now what do I do? Work, vacation, landscaping the yard, remodeling the back porch, all takes a back seat to the intruder Death. A widow can surely lose her way upon this detour. She loses her sense of direction and very often her ability to read directions, decipher a map or maintain a constant rate of speed. Sometimes she goes extremely slow, other times, too fast, or in some instances, refuses to proceed at all.

I believe we who travel upon this detour need to leave signs along the way that mark the danger zones. It is our responsibility to alert those behind us about the pitfalls and potholes. Along this road will be those who would take advantage of such a traveler and we must establish road blocks to them. But we must also place arrows here and there to point out the unexpected beauties if we will just look. Even a lake of tears can reflect blue skies. And flowers will come up from the seed of those upon the casket if they are cast upon fertile soil. The soil is fertile here along this journey. We can leave a trail for others to follow.

We do not know how long the detour lasts or where it comes out, but there is an ultimate destination ordained by God, and we need to be on the journey. The detours of our lives can be blessings we never dreamed possible, but if our heads are forever down, if our eyes are swollen shut by tears, we may pass the beauty unnoticed. Yes, we cry and hang our heads. But sometimes we need to look about, if only to get our bearings. Watch for the signs that others have been kind enough to leave, but be sure to leave some yourself. Maybe you should stop long enough to plant a seed of hope that will bloom another day.

When you arrive back to the main road of life, think on that detour. Do not forget about the others who will be forced to take it. Be patient with them if they do not catch up with you as quickly as you would like. If you have left your gifts of beauty along the way on that road, it will be more tolerable for them and affect their healing. The main road will never be the same again.

The memories will not end . . . the detour will.

Now I Get It

Now I get it. I've always heard about broken hearts and thought it was just an expression. Now I know that it is real. I wondered why I felt so empty inside. It makes so much sense now. When the heart breaks, it can no longer hold the contents of life. Those wonderful things that make up what life is about, spill out. The heart breaks when your husband dies. It splits into tiny shards and you are left to view the remains.

Just when I thought it was safe to go out; when I thought surely everyone around me knew he was gone, I took my car to be inspected and the attendant asked where my husband had been keeping himself.

When it had been five weeks, I thought I'd be much better after five months. Now, at five months, I wonder if five years will do it. How much time does a heart need? Where is the glue, the filler, the tape to hold it together? Dear God in Heaven, I miss him so. If an attendant at the inspection station notices him gone and misses him, how much more must I notice and miss him? I saw him every day, loved him, touched him; I needed him.

How can I get through this? I tell myself that so many others have been upon this path, and handled it gracefully. How poorly I am doing. I realize now that although we are set upon a path, that our moccasins do not necessarily glide over the stones and ditches along the way. We stumble, we fall, we bleed, but we continue on our journey. We carry this broken vessel we call a heart to the One who made it and respectfully hand it over to Him. We have no idea why it had to break, but we know we can trust Him with what is left of it.

So, if I sometimes appear to be fragmented, distracted, or different than I should be, please bear with me; I have once more handed over my heart to the Lord, and am doing the best I can in its absence.

A New Life

As I think of giving birth, agonizing pain is endured for the joy that the young one will bring. It is born through pain mixed with love. But that baby will not automatically place his arms around you and say, "Mama, I love you." There is a process through which we go to get to some point of reciprocation of our emotions. There are many sleepless nights, times when you cannot imagine what is wrong and you long for him to just tell you where he hurts or what you can do to make things right.

Slowly you adjust to this new life and find things within yourself you never knew existed; the strength to carry on.

When one is born-again, it is a pain borne by the hands, feet, and life of the Savior. His sacrifice has allowed you a new life and this time, *you* are the baby. There is much to learn and obedience takes on a new meaning. Although your legs can walk, there are times when you are unsure of which path to take.

Slowly you adjust to this new life and find things within yourself you never knew existed; the strength to carry on.

When a spouse dies, there is at least a part of you that also dies. You may feel you were buried with him. The pain is hardly bearable and the life you knew and loved is no longer possible. Just as we made the choice to start a family, and made the choice to give over our old life and begin with the newness given by our Lord, we now have the choice of allowing this pain to carve us into still another form. It is a difficult choice, for we cling so tightly to what was comfortable, beautiful, and so right for us. But as the young school child cries for leaving his mother and enters a world into which the mother can never go, so must we. We must go, even if it is tearfully into that new place where we learn and grow and become who we are supposed to be.

And slowly you adjust to this new life and find things within yourself you never knew existed; the strength to carry on.

Cast thy burden upon the Lord, and he shall sustain thee. Psalm 55:22

RUNNING ON EMPTY

I don't like the word loneliness. It sounds so pitiful. It doesn't feel right saying that I am lonely. I think of it more as empty. I have a sense of emptiness. Emptiness is:

How you feel when you sneeze and there's no one around to say "Bless you."

Seeing mistletoe and thinking of it as a parasite rather than a place to steal a kiss.

Having the whole day off and not having a clue how to spend it.

A queen size bed with no king in it.

A church pew where you cannot hear his song.

The night when he doesn't call you outside to view the stars.

The tree swing he hung with no one to push you.

Pasta for one.

Prayer with no one to take your hand.

Watching a funny movie with no one to laugh with.

Having a great thought with no one to tell it to.

Painting something without appreciation.

Finding out just how long a night really is.

No sound or movement in your house, but your own.

Emptiness is me. I am not just empty; I am spilled. How does one refill her life? How do I change the hollowness? The glass is not half full or half empty. It is empty. It even feels broken. Can it ever hold anything again?

I ask myself if this may be something akin to despair, but I think not. Empty is not despair. It is nothing. It is not joy, it is not sadness; it is just empty. Is a plateau high or low? Is the sun rising or setting at the exact moment of noon? How can I live if the mate of my soul has died? There is probably no answer to this, or even a comment worth making; it is just an empty statement.

What is the opposite of empty? Is it full? Is it one of those words like perfect? Nothing is more perfect, it is just perfect. Can one be *kind of empty?* I've heard of running on empty when one's car needed gasoline. Right now, I'm running on fumes with no idea how to refuel.

I am so glad that I can have these feelings and ask these questions knowing that my Lord knows all the answers even if no one else does. If no one else in the world could satisfy me with even one answer to any of these questions, I know that my Lord holds them all and just His presence is enough to fill the moment, even if it seems so very empty; He is in it.

Fall-ing

It is late summer, just on the cusp of autumn, and I am surprised at my ambivalence at the changing of the season. I am usually excited at the first chill in the air, observing the first leaf fly in the wind and the crunch of dry grass beneath my feet. The signs never change, but the circumstances do. This has always been my favorite time of year with anticipation of all the wonderful year-end events ahead. The very thought of the fragrance of wood smoke was a thrill.

This year, I shall be tucking away more than flower beds and summer clothes. I am trying to decide what to do with the clothes of my husband who no longer abides upon this earth. They still hang silently in the closet and fill the drawers. I guess it doesn't matter anymore what became of those missing socks or the stain I never could get out of his favorite tee-shirt. I have put off dealing with this since spring. Now summer has passed and another season approaches. I think it is more than a season of climate; of chilled air, or pumpkins and turkeys. It is a season of putting things away forever that will not re-emerge next spring. It is time to clean out his side of the closet and put his shaving things away. Just because it is time does not mean it is easy or that I will do it yet. Just touching his things is so hard for me. I am unsure where they belong. I want someone to get some good from his exquisite taste, but I am protective of them.

What if they don't take care of them the way he would have. His alligator shoes, his cashmere top coat, his sweaters that still emit his cologne; to whom do I entrust these treasures? Is there a rule or guide somewhere that helps a widow know these things? Oh God, how I miss him. How I miss these things on him, and around me!

The chill now is felt more inside than out. I can hope that something will light a fire within my spirit some time down the road and until then, learn how to tuck away those parts of my life that will never re-emerge. I shall not forget them, but I must find new kindling for new warmth and new fire. Though my resources are wet with tears, I know God can get it started. I always loved that little song my daughters used to sing, "It only takes a spark, to get a fire going." The spark will come when it is time for the fire to begin. Today I gather a piece of kindling, tomorrow, perhaps another. When the time is right, would you like to attend my bon-fire? Maybe it will help light the way for someone else such as I.

HEROES

When I was a young girl, there were two women I looked to with respect and admiration. I guess one might call them my heroes. They exuded grace, dignity, poise, charm, and style—all the things of which I felt devoid. I watched and studied them hoping somehow I might be able to duplicate some gesture or quality to which I aspired. It was a time when I didn't know who I was and so if I was going to invent myself, I wanted to replicate at least some of those qualities.

I am no longer that young girl, and those heroes are gone now. I am a widow in my early fifties, and I now wonder to whom I look to re-invent myself. When you aren't sure who or what you are, in what direction do you look for some clear picture?

I have observed the women around me and those spotlighted in the media, but I do not see anyone who possesses the essence of what I would want to be. I feel that I lost much of myself in the death of my spouse, and much of my grain has been sanded beyond recognition. I must once again find the right groove for myself. As I am no longer a wife, my focus is changed; as is my purpose for each day.

And so as I think on all the women, great and not-so, there is only one who comes to mind for me to emulate. According to the dictionary, the word means to try to equal or surpass; an attempt to excel, or rival successfully. Therefore, I must look to the woman I had become, assess her dimension, and proceed in surpassing that being. That woman was confident and comfortable in her womanhood. Right now, I feel I have become a silhouette with no defining features, but I realize also that this is temporary. I want to define each area of my face and life with vision, inhale fresh new air, and fill in the gaps with those qualities which I have always admired. So I look at myself and attempt to reunite my broken spirit with the things I respected and admired about the woman I had become. From there I may proceed to surpass and excel her with every new challenge and obstacle. My real hero is my Lord. He is the potter and I am His pliable clay.

Who do you want to be now that you are not defined by "Mrs."? It was a label in which I took enormous pride. It has been stripped and what is left? Please join my anticipation of what will be next in our individual personalities. We must become who we were always meant to be, with or without a title, or a spouse. That is the real essence of our womanhood. Look to the Lord. Follow His lead, and then be who you are supposed to be with all of your might.

A Gentle Touch

I awoke this morning to the softest touch of a hand upon my chest. It was hardly there at all, but such a very gentle touch. Before I opened my eyes to the experience, I smiled just slightly and then looked to see from where the gentleness had come. It was from my own hand.

Except for the hugs of sympathy in these months since the death of my husband, I have been touched very little. I think I have already forgotten the wonder a touch has in it. Of course there are no more wonderful kisses from my mate, no embraces, and anything resembling sex is quite out of the question. But there has to be something that feels good without committing oneself to sin, or even a promise.

Since I am the only one who will never leave me, except, of course, for my Lord, maybe a soft touch upon my cheek or so gently over my heart would be a nice thing to administer to myself. Maybe it is a good way to get in touch with my feelings, literally.

I must practice gentleness each day, and perhaps it should begin with myself. I can learn the art of tenderness from my own needs, from what I desire. Sometimes I wish someone would just come up to me and hug me, or touch my face, smile and then leave. Words seem so superfluous these days. Please don't ask me how I am doing. How am I *supposed* to be doing? The answer is, "I am doing the very best I can."

So, if I should walk up to you and touch you, smile, and then leave, just know that I am doing what I want someone to do to me. Isn't that a rule or standard to live by anyway? It sounds very golden to me.

THE LETTER

Dear Lee:

I need to talk to you so badly. Six months without telling you some new, exciting news or showing you the latest thing that I have painted or just sharing my hair-brained ideas with you is almost too much to bear. So, knowing how proud of me you would be for some new thing I conquer, I want to bring you up to date. Of course, it is possible that you are somehow aware of my every move, but I need to tell you anyway. It is sort of like praying. God already knows my heart, but praying is more for me than God.

I sold our bus that we loved so much. Since I couldn't drive it, and I wouldn't want to anyway without you in it; it didn't make sense to keep it. I put an ad in an RV magazine. I knew it would be a while before it would appear in the next issue, so I had time to detail it before showing it. It was bittersweet rummaging through it all, but I felt your presence so much in those close quarters. Knowing how you loved it made polishing the walnut a joy rather than a job. Shining the brass foot bar where you rested your feet mornings as you ate breakfast made me look up at happier days. The windows through which we viewed the beautiful lakes, hills, parks, sunsets and glories of our life together were a pleasure to clean.

And then the calls began with inquiries. Knowing you don't enjoy all the little details I am wont to describe, I shall simply say that six days after the ad appeared, the bus was sold. That's wonderful in itself, but the best part is the man who bought it committed for it, sight-unseen, over the telephone, wired the funds to the bank and didn't even try to lower the asking price. How about that? Did I do a good job? No; we both know that the Lord had His hand on the entire project. He is the only man in my life now, but you know, He is enough.

Now I want to tell you about my latest victory; and every day that I manage to get through without you is a victory. Well, I bought a trailer. I really needed more room for moving my artwork around to the shows that I do. So I purchased a used trailer and wouldn't you know, the light kit didn't fit, so I had to take it in for a new light system. I backed the Suburban up to it, connected the hitch and drove it right up to the dealer. How long it took me is another detail you don't want to know, but the point is, I did it! I kept it on; I didn't need the practice (ha ha), and probably won't remove it until all my shows are done. Yes, I drag it back and forth to the motel, but this morning, I backed that trailer up to the door of the coliseum and didn't hit anything or anybody. It's a good thing they don't count off for how long it takes me though. I would much rather be directing you into our spot, but that's not going to happen, so as I make up my mind that I have to take out the trash, bathe the dog, take care of the income tax, *create* the income; this too, I shall manage.

I have a sense of your presence, maybe because I am wearing your sweater, but it feels good to feel you. I know that God is protecting and providing for me and prompts me as I go. I'll be fine; I want to live a glorious life in joy and grace. It is always a challenge, even a greater one alone. But I seek it. You would expect that of me. When you were here I could not bear the thought of disappointing you. I still cannot.

Love,

Jan

Even Automatic Doors Don't Open if You Don't Approach Them

In the weeks and months following the death of my husband, I, myself, felt entombed. I had no idea why I was left to live without him. I had no sense of purpose. One Sunday morning, my pastor, Brother Rick Cundieff, used as his text John 11:39–40. In the text, he read, "Jesus said, Take ye away the stone. Martha, the sister of him that was dead, saith unto him, Lord, by this time he stinketh; for he hath been dead four days. Jesus said unto her, Said I not unto thee, that, if thou wouldest believe, thou shouldest see the glory of God?"

I find it interesting that Jesus told the woman to move the stone. Even as a mortal man, he would have been stronger than a woman in the moving of a stone, and being Almighty, He certainly could have done it himself. It occurred to me that our Lord would require of us actions of which we are capable, even if difficult or stressful. He didn't do it for her, but engaged her in the process of the miracle He would perform.

As I listened to this story of Lazarus that I have known since a small child, I related to it in a new perspective. Now, it was my husband in the tomb; and I had locked myself away in there as well. I did not know how to get out. That Sunday morning as Brother Rick spoke, my Lord told me to remove the stone and come out of the tomb; that if I would believe, that I would see the glory of God. Brother Rick said, "Even automatic doors don't open if you don't approach them." Wow! What a statement. I understood that it would be necessary to be up and about the business of healing and that taking that step of faith in the direction of the Lord would open doors. *I* had to do something to experience the miracles He wanted to perform. Hiding out in my house in the country behind closed doors would not do a thing.

It has been difficult pushing the stone away that I might live again. It seemed easiest just to hide away in my self-imposed grave and mourn, but there is no glory to God in that. As I enter the business of living again, I realize that I have almost forgotten how. From a previous study of the same scriptures, I had written a note in my Bible the words of my former minister, Steve Swofford, First Baptist, Rock-wall, who made a great point of the story. He asked the question, "What do you need done in your life that a God who can raise someone from the dead cannot handle?" Wow again! "Jan, come forth!" Loose me and let me go. Let me go forward and live the abundant life that God ordained for me. For the widows of the world, God will give us the strength to remove the barrier to what is keeping us from living again. He won't do it for us, but He will enable us in the doing of it.

The woman was right. Death stinks! We must inhale the fragrance of life again. Move the stone. Wash your face. Buy some flowers for the living room; yes, the *Living* room, buy a new dress, or scarf, or hat, or gown, or anything that is new. Seek newness of life in everything. "Come forth."

The Positives of a Negative

I recently received a letter from a friend telling me she had found an old negative she thought I would like to have developed. I held it up to the light and had difficulty determining what the picture might be. Black was white, and vice versa, and it was so dark, I couldn't really tell what I was looking at. Living in a small town, it is necessary to travel several miles to have film developed, so I wasn't sure it was worth the trouble to get it done.

It has been seven months since I buried my husband, and I feel very much like that negative. I can't really get a real picture of myself anymore. What used to be so clear is dark and difficult to decipher. What was white seems black now. What was so good seems to be very bad. I wonder if it is even worth the effort to pursue the picture of who I am now; now that my spouse is no longer in the picture.

Right now I am in a negative stage of life. Living in the shadow of the life we shared is safe for the moment, but I am profoundly aware that God is developing me into a new picture. I cannot see the background clearly, even the foreground, or the faces of those around me, but I am confident that He is developing a wonderful masterpiece for me. It is important to acknowledge that it is indeed worth the effort of having it done. I must make the trip trusting the outcome to my Lord. I do not feel photogenic, my eyes may be shut, but He is the master photographer and the picture is almost ready to leave the dark room.

Even the dark room can bring beauty. I must make something beautiful of this negative situation that I have been sent. I did not ask for it. I had no idea it was coming, but here it is. Develop it, look at it, pass it around, pass it on. I will show you my picture; send me yours when you have the courage to have it developed. Not only is God a master photographer; wait until you see the frame He is carving out for you; and try to smile; it's amazing how great it can feel.

Which Way Did She Go?

Sometimes I think I have misplaced my very self. I misplace my keys almost every day. I am sure that my purse has feet and that it plays hide and seek with me, and just now, I wanted my shawl for my shoulders to chase the chill of the morning, and it has hidden somewhere, refusing to be found.

To say that I am a bit distracted is an understatement. Having lost my husband to cancer earlier this year, I wonder what else I am missing that I don't even know about. At first I meant this literally, like maybe important papers, or even clothes or shoes. But now, as I think on it, I wonder what I may be missing by the distraction of circumstance. I shall never forget the beauty of our lives together; the gentle man with whom I walked, loved, lived. But I should not forget the woman that *I* am, and am supposed to be either. Even if I am not sure what I have done with her for the moment. I must not allow her to hide from me the way a second shoe does or some lost recipe. There is a place for me and I want to be there. The old saying, "A place for everything and everything in its place" hardly describes my life right now. What *are* those things on my desk anyway? But I know there is a place for me and it isn't hiding in the closet, or behind closed doors, or even in the past. What a dishonor to the love that we shared. What a dishonor to the woman my husband so loved.

As I attempt finding myself, I am not sure I shall recognize myself at first. I have experienced things lately I never dreamed I would be required to manage. But through it all, I hope that when I do find myself that I still remember how to smile, how to laugh, and how to live.

If you want, you are welcome to join me in the search. Just don't give up on me; I don't think I have ever been quite this lost before.

GAPS

I recently came across my high school graduation picture. I had forgotten about the large gap between my two front teeth. I recall how much I wanted braces to correct it. I hated my smile showing that gap. I wanted perfection, but I didn't get braces.

Through the years the gap has closed and my front teeth meet nicely together. I wonder had I gotten braces to bring them together if today I would need a retainer to keep them apart?

When my husband died, I experienced a gaping hole in my life. I thought nothing would ever fill it again. I hated my life showing that gap. The only braces available for this kind of gap are those from the Holy Spirit. Never mind what the smile looked like, there wasn't one. I wanted perfection. I got braces; braces that held onto me in that gap; that kept me not only where I needed to be but also where I would eventually go.

Today the gap is not nearly so wide as it was a few months ago. Just as little by little, without my notice, the gap closed between my teeth, so has the gaping hole in my life. God is filling me daily with such abundance and bounty that even I sometimes forget about the gap. The day will come when the gaping hole will be only a memory and I shall be filled again, and what a smile that will be!

TASSELS

The tassel on the book mark in my Bible came off this morning. I'm not sure if I ever saw how a tassel was made or what it looked like come apart. It was just a bunch of strings in a pile looking not at all like the pretty dangling thing it had been before. I suppose that describes me. I saw myself there in that pile of threads. Before my husband died, I seemed to have it all together. The many threads of my life; my husband, children, church life, career, hobbies, home, animals were all beautiful parts of the tassel that adorned my life.

But cancer has a way of cutting the binding and all the pieces fall to the ground. I look at them now, as I am trying to decide what to do. Do I just toss them away, or do I gather them up and hand them back to God? After all, these pieces of the tassel of my life were gifts from Him anyway. He can bind my wounds, and weave together what is left of the strands of me. He might even add some more strands. I like tassels. Now I know how they are made. They are made with the gifts of God. I am well-adorned.

Destination: Unknown

On the way to my desired destination this morning, the exit I needed to take was blocked off and I had to proceed on and find a new way to get to where I was going. Being in a strange place, a city I rarely visit, I had no idea what route to take. I am not known as a human compass anyway. I just plundered on and hoped my turns would be the right ones. Along the way I didn't notice the landscape, scenery or terrain because of my disappointment and disdain for the inconvenience of it all.

I arrived at my destination in tact with only a minor delay. It occurs to me that becoming a widow is much like coming to a detour in the road. Before my husband died, I knew where I was going, how to get there, with whom I would be traveling, and I thought I knew the way. Now I have been diverted from my known route, and I no longer am sure of where I am going, much less, how to get there.

I suppose I just watch for the signs from God, read His holy map every day, and depend on Him as my compass. Right now I feel like I am idling and not getting anywhere. Maybe now is the time to just "Wait on the Lord". I would love to mount up with wings as eagles and fly to some new destination where I am not confused by detours. God is going to take me to His grand destination, and I should learn to trust His navigation. I wonder where He is taking me. Wherever it is, I believe it will be a fine ride.

"But they that wait upon the Lord shall renew their strength; they shall mount up with wings as eagles; they shall run, and not be weary; and they shall walk, and not faint." Isaiah 40:31

FEAR NOT

There are 365 "Fear Nots" in the Bible. It is so obvious what conclusion we can draw from such a fact, but just in case someone misses it, I shall say it anyway. There is one "fear not" for every day of the year. Daily, we are to abstain from fear and take courage in the fact that our Lord loves us and cares for us.

A Sesselbahn is a system of overhead cables slung from lofty pylons fixed in rocky slopes of a mountain. On these cables, cars are hung which are electrically caused to slide up the cables. We must be willing to trust the Sesselbahn that God provides to hold us as we approach one fear and another. He is the overhead cable holding the beat-up bucket of our lives. He will transport us over to victory; yes, even to the very top of the mountain, if we but trust His cables to hold us. I want to live fearlessly. I want to have the courage to walk boldly into the day with joy and thanksgiving for the gift that it is. I am at a great precipice of my life. I shall not retreat from my fears. His cable will hold.

When I think on it, what have I really to fear? Emptiness still comes to mind. I can handle the battles and trials and desperate moments that life wields my way, but when the victories are won, when dangers are past, with whom do I rejoice, or rest, or celebrate? That is my fear, I think; that I shall have this sense of emptiness for the rest of my life. I am not quite sure how to fill myself; but I know someone who does, if I will but allow Him.

That is where the "Fear Nots" come in. I am not to fear *anything,* even the emptiness. Maybe for others it is financial worry, loneliness, or physical stress. The "Fear Nots" will fit any size fear we have. Nothing is too big for God. Therefore, daily we put on our armor of courage, pick up our shield of faith, and step boldly, well, maybe not always so boldly, but we do step out and salute the day with our efforts; one fear, one day at a time.

"For God hath not given us the spirit of fear; but of power, and of love, and of a sound mind." 2 Timothy 1:7

Widows Anonymous

"Hello, my name is Jan; I am a widow." This sounds like the beginning of an Alcoholic's Anonymous meeting. In a way, maybe I am an addict, too. I am addicted to the life I used to lead; the one with laughter, joy, plans, dreams, and a reason to live. I have heard of stopping one's old lifestyle "cold turkey" and how difficult it is. They say the pain is almost unbearable. I understand.

What do I do now that I cannot have my daily shot of laughter? What is the treatment for this kind of void? Alcoholics usually drink coffee by the pots full and smoke like a chimney, but what does a widow do to replace her habit of happiness?

I suppose it sounds too simple to refer to the "Serenity Prayer", but it seems to work for them; maybe it will encourage me "to change the things I can and accept the things I cannot." I definitely cannot change the fact that my husband is dead. Maybe I can change how I deal with it, or even how I go about living what is left of my life. I have trouble thinking of a reason to live. Where can I get a cup of serenity, or a drag of courage? If ever I needed my cup to run over, it is now, but not with coffee. How about a big hot cup of patience or maybe a dish of peace!

How do they end their speech when they finish? I think they say something like, "I haven't had a drink in seven months." Well, I haven't had a husband for seven months, and with the grace of God I am going to make it, "one day at a time." God help me.

Lost is a Four-Letter Word

I hate it when I lose something. I misplace things constantly. I forget what I am doing even as I am doing it. If my keys are missing, I get frustrated. If I can't find but one shoe to a pair, I whine, and if I misplace my wallet, I panic. Let's talk about really losing something; something that is gone for good. I won't come across it when I clean out my closet, and it won't just show up when I least expect it. When I lost my husband to cancer, I experienced all of these responses and more. If my keys are missing, they will turn up; after all, the car is in the drive; rather simple. I can always select another pair of shoes, or keep looking and the shoe will show up sooner or later; and except for the trouble of canceling credit cards, and having a new driver's license issued, no big deal. But losing a husband is entirely different. I cannot cancel cancer the way I would a credit card. I can't order a new spouse the way I would a driver's license. I can offer no one a reward for his safe return. He is lost to my daily life forever.

Today I had an appointment with my attorney to view the rough draft of my new will. Things must be changed when a mate dies. As I was attempting to get ready, I could not find my make-up bag. So I decided to go bare-faced. I am really getting courageous these days. Then, when the time came to leave, not only could I not find my keys, which is pretty common for me, but I could not find my wallet anywhere. I am quite surprised I even knew where the car was. Luckily my sister was at my house and she was able to deliver me to my appointment. She told me to call her when I had finished my business and she would come get me.

When we completed our corrections and got everything the way I wanted it, I dutifully called my sister and went outside to wait for her arrival. As I stood in front of the office, I decided it might be nice to just walk to the corner and watch for her there. When I got to the corner, I decided to walk across the street and wait. Well, just a few steps and I decided to walk in the direction from which she would be coming. Before I knew it, I had walked several blocks and actually arrived at my sister's house where her husband looked at me curiously, wondering where his wife was. I confessed I had gotten carried away with myself *again;* and now we had to find my sister, who by now was worried I had been abducted. One has to wonder what I could be thinking to behave in such a manner. Well, the answer is, I was not thinking; which brings me to the present moment. I am so thankful that the Lord is watching out for me and that He assigns guardian angels to His children. Wow! Mine deserves a bonus or an extra halo or a vacation, or something really special for taking on this assignment. I hear they are ten feet tall. That sounds so exciting to think that a ten foot tall warrior goes ahead of me, making sure I don't get lost along the way and brings me to the place where God intends me to be; even from the attorney's office.

"Behold, I send an angel before thee, to keep thee in the way, and to bring thee unto the place which I have prepared." Exodus 23:20

May I Serve You?

The first hurdle of the season is over. I survived the Thanksgiving holiday without drenching the household with tears. When the time came for everyone to recite those things for which they were thankful, I hesitated and just declared my thanks for survival. I hope I didn't seem ungrateful to those present, but I am quite certain my Lord knows my heart and understands my intent.

As I look about my house on this Monday morning, trying to make it at least *walk-throughable,* from all the neglect of the last several months, I find myself wishing that my emotions and psyche were as easily tidied as is my house. The cobwebs in the corner of the room cannot compare to the cobwebs in my heart. I want so much to actively love. It seems that love has taken on a passive state in my life, and I am stuck in the mode. I can remember not too long ago having a passion for so many things. Today my passion is a blank page. I wait for God to write upon that page where He wants me to be. For now, I have made arrangements to run away.

In the attempt to avoid any semblance of a traditional celebration of Christmas, I have opted for a mountain-top experience. To put it another way, I have accepted a position at a Colorado guest ranch in the capacity of dining room help. I have never been a waitress, or at least been paid for it.

I have served my children, husband, and guests in my home. Surely I can conquer this little task; at least for three weeks. Turning my attention to others, serving them and learning new things will surely be better than trying to make sense of tangled tree lights, ornaments collected over the years, and how long to cook the turkey. This way, I just serve what someone else has cooked.

In a way, that is exactly what I must do with this part of my life anyway. I must serve in spite of what has been cooked for me. Sometimes it feels like "my goose is cooked", but alas, I must view it as the appetizer to the feast God has prepared for me. Widowhood is not appetizing. It is ugly, unappealing, and not at all what I expected. It was not listed on the menu. It just got served to me. Now I must swallow it and digest what it means to me. I can allow it to make me sick, or use it to the nutrition of my soul. It will either give me food poisoning or strengthen me. It is my choice.

As the snow falls upon the mountains around the guest ranch where I shall spend my white Christmas, I remember that each flake that falls is unique, as am I. I also recall something I read that "no snowflake falls in the wrong place." I think that I am right where I am supposed to be now. I want to use each unique experience that falls upon me to make a wonderful new landscape. It is cold, yes, but God has lit a fire in me that no cold, not even the coldness of the grave, can penetrate.

"May I serve you?" "I've never done this before." "I haven't been a waitress *or* a widow."

That's What It's All About

I saw a sweatshirt today that said, "What if the hokey-pokey is really what it is all about?" Now that is a thought provoker if ever there was one. What is it all about anyway? Is it just "to put your right foot in, put your right foot out and shake it all about; do the hokey-pokey and turn yourself about?" Well, maybe so, depending on what the hokey-pokey actually is.

Sometimes we feel we are being turned all about, or being shaken to our very core. We place our feet upon one path and then another and still end up in the same place. Sometimes we put our right foot in, and then we put it out because we have no idea where it goes. Where do we place our feet; in what direction do we begin walking? As silly as the hokey-pokey looks when one is doing it, consider the widow doing it in the weeks and months following the death of her husband. Her life makes about as much sense as the song. She has no idea where to take the first step. She is dizzied by the dance and wonders what all of this is really about.

Life happens. Death happens. Somewhere in between we find someone with whom to dance for a while. We put things in, we take them out; we shake it all up and live with what we are given; and we live without when it is taken.

God is in charge here. I don't understand why my husband had to die anymore than I understand the words to that silly song. I just know that life isn't hokey; it's beautiful and wonderful and we must dance to it every chance we get. We must love our dance partner with passion and joy. And when he is no longer in the dance, we either sit it out, get another partner, or twirl alone across the dance floor of life. Maybe it's not so much as, "Do the hokey-pokey," as it is to just *do*. Do something. I notice that before you can put your foot *out,* that you must put it *in*. Maybe that is what it really is all about. Put into life what you can. What you take out is an extension of what you put in. Don't just stand there, do the hokey-pokey. Turn yourself about, twirl, dance, laugh, be silly, giggle, feel again. Yeah, that's what it's all about.

Fog

I recently encountered an extremely heavy fog on my way home from a business trip. It occurred to me that my life is pretty much in a fog right now, too. I noticed that I could hardly see a thing to my left or to my right and the view before me was extremely limited. Since my husband died, my perspective on things has totally changed as has my ability to see things clearly. I have no idea where I am going.

I feel like I am driving in a heavy rain without the windshield wipers operating. I can see nothing ahead and am so vulnerable to everything out there. I am reminded of the phrase, "Don't look down" spoken to those in a high place. Now I know why; because I need to be looking *up* to my Lord for courage and safety.

In the midst of the fog, it is difficult to appreciate the beauties around me, but I acknowledge that they are there and that one day the fog will lift and once again I shall thrill to the landscape and those in it. I should take things very slowly, as anyone else in a heavy fog would normally do. I watch carefully and stay prepared to stop suddenly if anything or anyone comes too closely. These are safety measures right now. The time will come when I can pick up speed and see more clearly. Slow down, watch carefully, don't get too close to anyone (at least for now), and know that when the sun shines through that blinding fog of pain and sorrow, there is a beautiful world out there to drive through and enjoy.

Don't look down; look up to God. Don't look back; look up to God. You won't fall, or at least if you do, He will catch you in His loving arms and put you back on the most wonderful track. Use this fog right now to prepare for what is ahead. You even have a built-in excuse for cautious behavior. You are learning to drive solo which brings to mind the thought of flying solo. Maybe I'll learn to do that next. For now, I am waiting for the fog to lift.

"Oh that I had wings like a dove! For then would I fly away, and be at rest. Lo, then would I wander off, and remain in the wilderness. I would hasten my escape from the windy storm and tempest." Psalm 55:6–8

Just a "Swangin"

There is a swing hanging from a giant oak tree in the middle of my property. My husband hung it there years ago. We used to go out there together and sit and talk and swing. Our dog would join us as she always wanted to be where we were. It was a lovely thing we did; a simple and lovely thing.

Now I go to that swing alone and talk to God and watch the sunset and think of sweeter days. I still feel my husband's presence in the breeze as I swing. I hear the rustle of the leaves beneath his feet as he would stand behind me and give me a gentle push. I am comforted by the easy glide and the lift that he left me with. In so many ways, he still gives to me each day. It does not make me cry, but thankful and proud to have been loved so completely by such a man. It is a miracle people find one another that are so perfectly suited for each other, but our God is a God of miracles. And God is working more miracles for me; even those I do not yet know about. I know He protects and provides for me. He is the man in my life now and it is enough.

Recently our pastor did an acrostic on the word love. "L" was for the light God provides to His children. "O" is for the optimism we can have in being His children. "V" is for the victorious life we can have through Him and the "E" is for eternal life. That is wonderful and very true. But

I think that the "E" also stands for enough. In my life as a widow, although I am not wealthy, the Lord is my provider, and has blessed me that I don't have to worry about finances. He will provide for me, and it will be enough. I don't have to worry about relationships; He is enough. How could I ever doubt His love just because I do not understand what is going on? When I sit in that swing, placing my weight on it and push off into the air, I expect it to hold me. I expect the same thing from my Savior right now as I place this enormous weight upon Him. It is enough. He is enough.

I want to swing high before the chariot "swings low to carry me home." I believe it is what the swing and I were meant to do.

Surgery without Anesthesia

It is easy to intellectualize pain
when it is someone else's.
Life performs surgery without anesthesia and we are embarrassed by the screams.

Miracles

Is there such a thing as a small miracle? In the months since the death of my husband, I have been the recipient of so many blessings and witnessed many miracles on my behalf.

While driving along the highway on my way to visit my daughter and her family, one of my tires just exploded. I pulled over immediately, and before I could even turn off the key, a man pulled behind me and offered to change the tire. He would not allow me to pay him, and although I insisted nothing could persuade him. I did something that seems crazy now that I think on it, but I just stepped over to him and hugged him. When he left, I was convinced that the guardian angel God has assigned to me indwelled his body.

I went to purchase a new tire in a different town from where I had bought the damaged tire. I figured I would have to buy a new tire and take the shards of the other tire to the original dealership. In fact, the two technicians who waited on me told me so. As I stood beside my vehicle waiting for them to remove what was left of the rubber from the rim, a young man walked up to me and asked, "How may I help you?" I replied, "Well, they are changing a tire for me. Would you like to see what happened to it?" When he saw the tire in the rear of my Suburban, he just picked it up and removed it. As he walked off, he said, "Ma'am, I can handle the adjustment for you right here."

Maybe it is a small thing to some, but to me, it was a miracle. The miracle of God sending gentle and helpful souls to me to fill in where there is no longer a husband. For all the bad in the world, for all the ill treatment that we hear about; hear this as well. There are wonderful saints among us. Hebrews 13:2 tells us, "Be not forgetful to entertain strangers; for thereby some have entertained angels unawares." I met two of them in twenty-four hours.

If I stopped to think of how vulnerable I feel in this big world, I would probably never leave home. But I need to be about the business of living. I will go to see my grandchildren, assume some semblance of work, and step out on faith that my Heavenly Father indeed watches over me. He expects me to use good judgment and not take unnecessary chances, but He continually sends wonderful people across my path to bless me, and sometimes, more often than I could even guess, I believe He sends angels. I am humbled by His watch-care and encouraged as well. I do wonder how and where they hide their wings.

LEARNING

I am sitting at the computer I have recently acquired trying to function as a member of modern society. If someone were to enter the room right now, he would probably think I knew what I was doing. He would be very wrong.

I have probably selected a terrible time in my life to learn something new; something as difficult as making friends with a computer anyway. But, it seems very safe and impersonal, which to me, right now, is very desirable.

Several months ago I acquired a new label. I am called a widow. I used to think that word was only for elderly women who should realize that it was the natural order of things for a husband to die. I never thought it would happen to me. I am learning all kinds of new things these days. I actually backed up my vehicle and attached a trailer onto the hitch. I placed an ad in a periodical and sold a bus that I knew nothing about, except that the driver was gone. I have found the courage to approach our banker without fear and trembling. Our CPA even told me what a good job I did preparing the details for him to do our taxes.

I, however, have not learned how to get through even one day without crying. I haven't mastered sleeping an entire night, or just for an instant, hoping that the call is from him when the telephone rings. I really don't know what to think of myself in terms of society today. I am not sure where I belong. The closest thing I can think of is "Married: With No Husband". I do not feel single. It is difficult to feel married without a spouse. Maybe the truth is I just don't feel much of anything. There are truly no words to describe this location to where I have been taken.

So, as I sit staring at this screen, wondering what I am supposed to do next to get it to work right, I could ask the same thing about myself. Maybe as I learn how to deal with this monster in front of me, the monster of despair will back off. Perhaps the monster of emptiness will pick on someone who is not wrapped up in figuring out how to file her latest page of thoughts. I shall probably learn very slowly as I do seem to be severely distracted, but I will learn. I will not fear this tower; I will not fear this Cyclops; I will not fear what I do not yet know.

Today it is a computer mountain I must climb. Tomorrow it may be a real mountain. I shall accept the challenge. Just as I must accept what my husband's death means; I must accept what my life means. It is to live as God has ordained. Now, *that* is something worth learning.

Changing Plans Again

Three days before I was to have left for my three-week job in Colorado, a blizzard blasted the very area I was to have entered. What was I thinking? Rain-slick streets scare me; how could I have even considered driving in mountains with snow and ice? Well, the answer once again is; I wasn't thinking.

Since I am not going to Colorado, I shall use these warm December days constructively. I need to paint my picket fence around the house. The filter on the heating system could use replacing, and I think I will rearrange the furniture in the house. I need to rearrange the furniture of my life as well. I am not sure anymore what goes where. For someone who used to be so into decorating, I don't even care if my sheets match anymore.

I suppose part of my problem is that I wonder what the use is of painting a fence, fluffing a pillow on the couch, or lighting a candle. I am not sure which comes first, the feeling or the stimulus to create the feeling. If I am ever to feel again, I think I should go ahead and light a fire, dream of a better day, and run naked in my mind. I say that because I seem to have hidden from my true self in mourning clothes. I want to shed them. I shall never forget the beauty of my life with my husband, but he would not wish me to forfeit what is left of my own. This would dishonor us both.

So, let me move the chair of despair, the couch of mourning and open the shutters to the sun. There is much dusting to be done; and considerable trash to discard. It's a start; that is all I am capable of now; starting.

THAT FIRST CHRISTMAS...
THIS FIRST CHRISTMAS

There are all kinds of firsts. It is December twenty-second and as I think on the birth of my Savior, I realize I am to look deeply into that manger scene and discover new truths. For one thing, I am quite certain that Joseph and Mary did not wish to make that trip to pay taxes, but they did what they had to do. The entire situation was most inconvenient, and poor accommodations did not help either. But this was all a part of God's plan, and they were obedient; the holy child was born, and the world was changed forever. What a wonderful first Christmas!

Now I find myself with another Christmas story; the one I live this season without my husband. I assure you this is one journey I, too, did not wish to take. Death does not consider convenience. It just comes and you are required to accommodate it as best you can. A baby born of a virgin is something I shall never be able to understand; I just accept it. A man I loved and adored, dying while still very young and in love with life is something I shall never understand either. Understanding is not the key to life, but acceptance might be.

This is the first Christmas without my husband beside me. It is possible that I shall become melancholy at times, but I need to remember that I am to celebrate a birth, not lament a death. If I can manage to do this, I shall benefit from this Christmas as well as from that very first Christmas.

As I run away to the beach to be alone with my Lord and my memories, I seek healing, peace and a new hope. And that is what Christmas brought the world after all, isn't it? Merry Christmas! Happy Holy Days! Celebrate a life born, celebrate a life lived, and celebrate a life left to live!

BEACH DAYS

You can't run from your troubles and problems; everyone knows that. Tomorrow my husband will have been dead eight months. I have come to the beach to be alone. The idea of celebrating Christmas in any traditional way was brutal to me. I am fortunate that my children understand my need for solitude. I have no idea how I shall celebrate this day next year or ever again, but for now, it is the only way that makes sense.

The healing process is different for each one of us; just as is the circumstance that brought us to the need for healing is different. I am at my best alone, I think. It is then that I have to take charge of things and not depend on others to meet my needs, emotional or otherwise. I become lazy in the presence of those who would tend me. They want to feed and nurture me, and although it is a lovely thing, and I am grateful for their intentions, there are things that must be done that only I can do. It is time to be alone with my Lord, coming to grips with what has happened and how best the two of us will get on with the life He has given me to live.

I have rented a house right on the beach. I will celebrate the birth of the Savior and salute the wonderful years of love and fun that my husband and I shared. He loved to bring me gifts all year long. He would see a crystal heart and bring it to me. He would take my hand and guide me outside to see the stars on a perfect night. Everyday was a gift and my mate was the sweetest expression of the very word "gift." He loved me and was never intimidated about showing me. He loved that everyone knew he was totally committed to me, absorbed in me, silly in love with me. What a joy to have loved and been loved like that.

This is what I think of now in these beach days. I wanted to see the sun, feel it, walk in it, run in it, be warmed by it. I wanted to walk the sand looking for simple treasure. I have found it here. I have not run from anything this Christmas. I have come apart from the bustle of what the holiday often becomes. I haven't over-eaten, gotten exhausted from preparations, or been overwhelmed by all that had to be done. I have simply come away with God. I love my family, but if I am ever to heal, I must be alone to tend my wounds and rest from it all. My weary spirit did not need to observe the goings-on of holiday joy. I have made my own version of it here, alone.

I believe I shall return to the reality of living, a stronger and happier woman than when I left. I am getting to know again the woman my husband loved. I think he would be proud of me; and I believe the Man for whom we celebrate this day will be too. That's a very nice gift.

The Dream

The dream was so vivid, so real, as the man who had been my husband spoke to me during the night before Christmas. It was a beautiful gift that I needed desperately.

"Jan:

First, I must tell you that I love you. You know I always started and ended with that when I was your husband. But my love now exceeds the boundaries of marriage. I now know what perfect love is. I have good teachers here within the walls of Heaven.

"My love for you has no ego or sense of possession; it is pure. I want what is best for you, just as our Lord does. I think you are doing very well. I do wish you would not cry so much, but tears can be very cleansing to the spirit. You are strong enough to continue your dreams without my physical presence. When the Lord told you that He would never leave you or forsake you, He meant it. I am witness daily to His love and faithfulness toward you as you go about mending your wounded heart. He makes sure your guardian angel has all he needs and I have actually seen our Lord smile when He speaks of how you are getting along. He loves you very much.

"Get back to reading His word, Jan. I know you feel confused over your interpretation of the scriptures. You believe your faith should have healed me. There are so many things I cannot tell you; not that it is forbidden, but there are just no words that translate to the language understood on earth. But when you arrive in this wonderful place, you will understand and you'll look at me and we will laugh together again. For now, you do indeed "see through a glass darkly," but the day will come when there will be no veils, no tears, and no broken spirit. I am whole again; and eternity is the ultimate marathon. I don't even need a sweat band anymore.

"I understand God has many wonderful things in store for you, and I am excited for all the joy it will bring you. I know you miss me. I know our children and grandchildren miss me too. Think of me all you want to, but do it in joy, not sorrow.

"Thank you for staying in touch with my mother. She has much to learn about love and you can teach her. Dad is here. We see each other from time to time, but it is a big place and there are so many wonders to perform, to witness and experience. God must have made eternity just to have time to do it all. We'll speak of Heaven when you are here, but you need to concern yourself with where you are right now. Don't feel guilty for any feeling you may have. We had a beautiful life together and no one could have made me happier. But I am not your husband now. I am your brother. You always wanted your brother to look out for you and support you and be there when you needed someone. Well, of course, you always had Jesus, but now you have me as your heavenly brother. The Holy Spirit allows our perfect love to accompany it when necessary. I have seen your tears enough. If our love was what I believe it was, then it is time for you to seek love in new forms. It does not have to be a man. It can be reaching out to other widows who can't seem to function in the absence of their own husbands. It might be a ministry you never imagined. God has this plan for you that even we in Heaven are not privy to; at least not the specifics. But we hear the angels talking among themselves and the word is that you are in for true joy.

"You are doing some unconventional things (and why would that surprise me?), and I think it's great. I can see that they are helping you. The beach for Christmas was a great idea. I understand what you are doing and I approve. I just want to remind you to trust the Lord in all you do and don't try to understand all of this. You won't. Wouldn't you hate it if you had been the one to make this trip first and I stopped reading my Bible? Wouldn't it bother you that I hide out in the balcony at church? I know you love the Father, and you know He loves you. Stay in touch. I hear your pleas, your petitions and prayers to God. Don't ask, "*Why,* God?" but ask, "*What,* God?" Seek Him with all you are and you will find all you need.

"Keep praying for our lost friends; I'd like to see them get through the gates. Not just for eternity, but for the joy of knowing our Lord can bring to their lives on earth.

"When you walk on the beach, you can remember the wonderful times we shared on that shore, but don't spend all your time looking back. Make new footprints, find new treasures in the sand, and enjoy each new sunrise. I am part of the color in it now. It is one of my favorite parts of Heaven. So many saints gather at sunrise and sunset and watch in awe at the Master's brush strokes. He uses us as His pigment. That is why no artist can reproduce the majesty of it. It is made of perfect love; perfect love that passes all understanding.

"When you call upon the Lord, the loud speaker vibrates Heaven. Your prayers are powerful; use them carefully; use them often, but use prayer, Jan. It is your key to life's joy. It is the passage to hope.

"You are well on your way in the healing process and I am pleased. Help others find their way to healing. I just thought I needed to say these things to you on this first Christmas since I came *home.* People were afraid you'd fall apart, but I knew better. You are wonderful. I always thought so, and still do. I am proud to call you my sister, and thankful to have been your husband. Now get on with your beautiful life.

Lee"

When I awoke from this dream, I inhaled a breath of peace. Sweet dreams.

HAIR GROWS BACK

I love my hair long. For most of my life I have worn it that way; but every so often I would get it cut and usually regret it. I would suffer through the growing out stage hating it all the way. I didn't even feel like myself during that time, but the day would come when I again could put it up or pull it back and I was *me* again.

My husband would often tell me, "Hair grows back, Jan," when I made decisions I regretted. He didn't want me to overreact to circumstances, in or out of my control. If things went wrong and I had trouble getting over whatever it was, he would say, "Jan, hair grows back." He wanted me to know that things would come out okay; but I needed to exercise patience.

I am trying to apply this simple wisdom to my life right now. It's considerably more serious than a bad haircut or an error in my checkbook. My husband is in the grave and I don't feel like myself anymore. So what do I do? I believe I need to exercise patience as this pain grows out. The growing out may take considerable time, but I get frustrated over the slow process of it all.

Things will someday be okay for me again; I know it. Grass will cover the grave. Yes, hair grows back, but it does so slowly. One cannot actually see it growing, rather the result of the growth. That is what I expect; that through this experience I will most likely not be aware of the daily growth. It will not be obvious to the naked eye, but one day I shall look up and observe that I have experienced real and tangible growth.

I hope you will like my new style. The cut almost killed me.

The Treadmill

I have a treadmill on which I walk about seven miles a day. At least that is my intention. Some days I do, other days, I don't. People use the word treadmill to indicate that they are not getting anywhere and for a while I compared my life since the death of my husband to being on a treadmill. But I have noticed that if I am disciplined about using it everyday that slowly, things get better. I can't tell by looking at first and for a good while nothing seems to change. But then one day I put on a skirt and it fits better than before. My pants are not so tight and I have better endurance when I encounter a physical task.

It does begin to show in small and wonderful ways. I have been on this treadmill for almost a year now. In the early days I could hardly stand from the pain of it, but I held on. I turned the speed way down, but I was there hoping things would change. The fatigue was more than I could bear at times and I would stop and decide to give up. But soon I would return to the thing and the exercise of the moment would help pass the time and somehow I would feel a little stronger for having stayed the course. Some days I would believe I was ready for a faster pace and almost fall on my bippy. Other days, things just came together and I could handle whatever I had to do with style and grace. Slowly the muscles were toned up and strengthened so that I could carry a little more weight upon my heart every day.

Sometimes it seems we are getting nowhere as we push on, but one day we look up and we are stronger, feeling better and able to handle the disciplines of living a little easier. Today I am stronger than I was ten months ago but not as strong as I want to be. I can face a new day without despair. I can face a task without the sense of uselessness. I do not yet feel energized about life but am experiencing new sensations of hope, and from time to time have actually caught myself enthusiastic about something. The treadmill can prepare us for new experiences and we will look back and know that for a while it was good to stay in one place while getting stronger. Some run out looking in all the wrong places for a quick fix and there are none.

Today I will step on my treadmill and walk seven miles. When I get off, my circulation will be better; I will be energized and my clothes will fit a little better. The treadmill I have been on in the regeneration of my spirit is beginning to show evidence as well. If you feel you are not getting anywhere and just marking time, please be patient. The day will come when the work you do on this treadmill; prayer, communication with the Father, reading uplifting materials, self-examination, even your tears, will reveal to you the new woman you are to be. This can be very exciting. Despair is a demon that Satan uses to thwart the spirits of the saints. Right now, out loud and with all the authority you can muster in your voice, declare, "Demon of despair, be removed from my life today and forevermore; in the name of Jesus I demand you remove yourself from my presence." Then be on with your wonderful life that God wants to use.

His Way Mine

Disappointment is a tricky thing. It sounds much better to say that I am disappointed than to say that I am pouting because I didn't get my way. When you boil it all down to the bottom and look closely at the dregs, that is usually the case.

I prayed with my whole heart for God to heal my husband of cancer and to spare his life. When things didn't go my way, I told myself I was dealing with the disappointment and heartache of having him no longer beside me. To a certain extent, that is true; but after a while, the painful truth is that I want what *I* want and think I know what is best for me, and in some cases, for others as well.

Before another crisis happens, before another time for strong faith beckons, I need to remember that when things are not going *my* way, that it is okay, because when I have God's hand on my life, things are going *His* way, and even though I don't understand it, or like it, that it is good. In fact, it is best for me.

When things are not going my way, I need to practice thanking God that they are going His way, and then stand back and watch all the wonders appear. When I was a little girl, one of my favorite songs I learned at camp was "His way Mine". I need to recall the words to that wonderful song when things are not going my way and be content that the creator of the universe is looking out for me. Way to go, Jan.

The Soil of Hope

When something wonderful happens in my life, I plant a magnolia tree. I have planted them in honor of weddings, the birth of my grandsons, new homes, and many occasions for celebration.

One of the magnolia trees is dying. There was a time when I would have been very disturbed over the fact that it will have to be replaced. It happens to have been planted for my first grandson and it is very dear to me. We have many photos of him standing beside it recording his growth as well as the tree's. I don't know why it is dying; it is just doing it right before my eyes and there is nothing I can do about it.

The magnolia is an evergreen with big, beautiful, glossy leaves and wonderful, white fragrant blooms. It is my favorite tree. It grows slowly but is strong and represents stability to me. But its strength is not exempt from disease and even with the best of care, it can die.

When I had to stand helplessly by and watch my husband die, unable to save him with the best love and intentions in the world, I realized the true meaning of helplessness. I put him on a special and disgusting diet, poured all kinds of tonics and miracle potions down his throat, and removed from his diet anything that might harm him; you know, all the things he loved. I read into the wee hours of the morning of possible approaches as to how he might be saved. Tea did not do it. Diet, medicine, radiation, hospitals, doctors, nurses, hospice did not do it. He just lay right there and died in front of me. I tried to make some sense of it all but I couldn't. I never will. I don't know yet how to really look upon that time with any wisdom gleaned or lessons learned. I suppose we just find out that when a thing happens, the only choice we have in the matter is how we shall deal with it and trust our Lord's wisdom above our own.

My husband's love was evergreen with a big glossy smile across his face all the time. I miss his magnificent fragrance. He was my favorite person in the world. There was no one whose company brought me more joy on this earth. Our love grew slowly and became stronger by the day and our relationship represented stability in my life I had never known existed until God gave him to me. But even in the strength of such love, he was not exempt from disease, and he died.

I can dig up the dying magnolia tree and replace it. It won't be the same, but it will be fine. However, one doesn't just replace a spouse like a tree that didn't survive. I have learned not to make such a big deal out of things that aren't big deals. A couple of years ago I would have lamented for days over the loss of the tree. Today, it just isn't that important. I recently had a tire disintegrate while driving along a highway. I called my daughter and told her that I had had a flat tire, that a kind man had stopped to change the tire and that I would be delayed. She marveled at my calm. When she commented on it, my response was, "It's just a tire." I am not sure I have learned how to live very well without the presence of my husband in my life, but I am learning that things are just *things*.

Before long I shall be digging a hole for another magnolia in honor of another grandchild, but I also hope the day will come when I shall have many more reasons to plant a magnolia. I hope to plant a forest of blessings. Life is precious. Celebrate it, plant it, grow it, nurture it, smell it, climb it.

DATE NIGHT

It seems so clear about how to behave myself during the day when the demands of the moment are upon me and the sunshine does its best to cheer me. When I speak to others on my progress in healing I try to be upbeat and positive. They are satisfied that I am surviving and that they have done their good deed for the day in making the contact. And even the nights are tolerable as the day ebbs into darkness and a book becomes my best friend or the crackle of the fireplace warms the room as well as my spirit. A call from a friend can pass the time magically, and there is always music to massage my mind if all else fails. But on a Saturday night when all the world seems to be in its date-night mode, a book is not always a friend, there is no phone call and the music seems melancholy, no matter the beat. I don't feel lonely; I feel wasted. For all the things I attempt doing throughout the week to make a contribution to my fellow man or my own needs, the hour arrives when I feel like a fraud. How am I really doing if I allow the calendar to affect me so? Why should Friday or Saturday night be any different from Tuesday night? I think we have programmed ourselves to the weekend being special.

I could bathe the dog, but it is winter and she would either freeze outside or she could wreck the bathroom. I could rent a movie but it might be funny, or sad, and with whom do I laugh or cry? I could work, or paint or read, but the fact is that I can't get my mind off the programming in my head that the night should be special. How can I make nights special now that there is no one special in them? I am confident that as a Christian that I should think of something like visiting the most special one in my life, that being the Lord. As much as I love Him, sometimes I just want something more tangible. Maybe that isn't very spiritual sounding, but He knows my heart and I can't fool him . . . or myself.

Perhaps I will invent something for these moments; like a game for one; something that sounds more cheerful than "solitaire." That even *sounds* lonely. But I like the idea that my efforts might assist another who has these Friday and Saturday night blues. There was a time when my husband and I ate out almost every weekend or went to a movie, visited friends or just sat and talked and laughed. Where does one use that energy as a widow? At my age, I am not yet content to think of myself as just a grandmother or widow or whatever label would assign me to some particular passive behavior. It all sounds so pitiful: the widow's lonely weekend saga. It isn't like that; I shall not be content to allow that to be the case; but what? A voice within reminds me, "Be still and know that I am God. I am God of the moment, God of your life; which means your feelings and needs. I am God of Friday and Saturday nights. Wait on me and not only will your weekends be blessed, but all the days of your life. I love you and know you better than you know yourself. This time will pass, and you will be stronger and happier that you waited as patiently as you were able to do for the blessings; and I have so many planned for you. You must believe this. You will be amazed at the joy you are destined to receive and know. Be still my beloved child and know that *I* am God, not you, or your feelings, but I. Delight yourself in me and I will give you the desires of your heart, when it is time."

So, that does it. Come on Friday night, I am ready for you. Saturday night, you cannot hurt me. My God is in charge of you and if I am here alone with myself, it is because He made the date, and I am in great company.

GIFTS

The house is full of activity and love. My grandsons are here playing with their holiday loot. They seem to try playing with all of it at once. They run from one thing to another. They are wonderful teachers. Life has so much to offer on every hand and I find myself allowing it to slip by because I am trying to heal from the wounded heart of widowhood.

Somehow I have adopted the idea that I am incapable of getting on with my life until some due course of time has passed; like one year. I have noticed that true survivors, and yes, victors, pull themselves up from bloody knees, broken limbs, wounded spirits and get back into the stream of life. What am I waiting for to access happiness? Do I feel the need to punish myself for having survived my spouse? Do I fear society will not nod with approval at my behavior?

God help me be like those dear children. They are given wonderful gifts and they go about enjoying them. I have been given gifts that I won't even open. The gifts are there for me to enjoy, but I put them away as if there were a more proper time to use them. It makes me think of those who would save a favorite dress for an occasion that never comes. I want to tear into life and enjoy the gifts my Lord has blessed me with.

Time is precious to me now. Somehow I thought I had this unspoken promise of many more decades to stroll through this life of mine. The death of a spouse can be like reveille, sirens and alarms all going off at the same time. It is time to get up, get started, and get your world turning. You may get a little dizzy at times, and for a while want to return to safety, but there really are no safe places, except the grave. That is not an option. Pick up the boxes, shake them, untie the ribbons and bows. Open your life up to new wonders.

GRETA COMES HOME

My dog, Greta, comes home today. She has been visiting my daughter and her family for almost three months. The nature of my work requires that I travel extensively during the months of October and November, and this being the first Christmas since the death of my husband, I stayed home very little in December.

I have been to see my best friend. She has been my best friend since we were about five years old. The summer I turned twelve bonded us in a relationship that would forever bless us. Although she lives in Florida, a thirteen hour drive from my door to hers, we have maintained our friendship through correspondence, phone calls and visits. It has survived distance, child-bearing and rearing, heartaches, disappointments, marriages, and now the death of my spouse. It is a source of strength on which I depend knowing that it is a direct gift of the Lord and I know He uses her to comfort and encourage me. I am grateful for Helen Anne Bruner in my life.

I have also been at the business of keeping the proverbial wolf away from the door through the abilities that the Lord has given me in my artwork. It requires strength only possible through His provision. The lifting, hauling and loading of the entire process is very difficult, as are the long hours in motels by myself. But I am thankful that this avenue is available to me for it allows me the freedom to pursue other considerations for my future that a limiting, regular job would not. I am blessed.

Christmas at the beach was very healing. It was very simple; no last minute runs to the mall, no frenzy. Christmas eve I sat on the deck of the beach house watching the day siphoned into the horizon. As the evening chill soaked into my body, I returned to the warmth of the room from which I could still witness the beauty of the shore. Standing in the kitchen, preparing simple fare, I often looked up at the glow of it. I wanted to cry and laugh at the same time.

After nibbling upon my tiny feast, I sat in front of the blazing fire and read the Christmas story out loud from the second chapter of Luke. I love the story of our Savior's birth. Then I gave thanks and as the fire continued to diminish, I spoke audibly to God about that first Christmas, and this first Christmas. It was a fine hour. I was given peace on earth for the first time in a long time and what an unexpected and beautiful gift.

The New Year is upon us and it looks as if Y2K will not play any major tricks on us. What I know is that Greta comes home today and it symbolizes getting back to the business of living. She has been such a good sport to have been farmed out. She has most likely enjoyed the experience because she adores my grandsons and they love her. But she is my reminder that it is time to join the land of the living and be about everything that that implies. I must take her tomorrow for her booster shots. I must get my house and heart in order for the new millennium. I cannot do it looking back at the heartaches of the past year. God uses what He will to perform His plan for our lives. Today he uses a ten-year-old Rottweiler. What a gentle teacher she is. Her total and perfect love for me, even when I avoid her for months at a time, is wonderful. She will still run to me and accept me for who I am and love me with no reservations. She will sit beside me, watch over me, and stand ready to ward off any harm that might befall me. She is loyal and faithful, even if I am not. Sounds very much like my Lord. He blesses me with love from all around. There are so many who want to close the gap created by the grave, and I must allow them to do it.

Greta comes home today, and so do I.

BLUEBONNETS

It is a frosty cold morning, and taking out the trash was the last thing I wanted to do. But I dutifully bundled up in my husband's warmest jacket (it seems men have jackets for warmth, women, for style), and dragged the trash can to the road.

On my way back to the house, looking down to keep the wind from my face, I noticed little plants appearing along the edge of the driveway. My husband loved bluebonnets and we did all we could to encourage their growth and reproduction. Our fields were quite prolific with large patches of them, and we gloried in their beauty in early spring. Our mowing took on rather strange patterns because we would not endanger even one beautiful bonnet until they went to seed, and then, mowing them was also the casting of seeds.

This past summer, I had our driveway filled in with gravel as it has continually washed out little by little for several years. The dump truck delivered several loads of ground granite and the bulldozer graded it nice and smoothly, and widened the area. Traversing the long drive is now smooth and has no ruts.

Those little plants I noticed, emerging through the layers of gravel and granite, were tender shoots of bluebonnets. Glory be to God! He may as well have spoken in an audible voice. The message of the Holy Spirit was loud and clear.

"Jan, although you buried your husband's body, nothing can bury the memories, nothing can cover what he loved, and all the beauties the two of you shared are still available to you. The bluebonnets he loved every year were not the same plants, but they are from the same seed and root system. And now as you continue on your journey, be it *to* the road or *down* the road, remember that no bulldozer, not even the dozer of death, can stop the bloom of his effect on others. No gravel or grave can bury the gifts he gave to you; and just as these tender shoots will survive, so, too, will you. It will be more difficult for them than those in the field, but some will go on to bloom. Jan, you must not only survive this massive bulldozer, you must bloom. Your life can bloom more beautifully than ten thousand fields of bluebonnets."

Right now, spring seems far away. The frost covers roof tops and it sometimes covers my spirit as well. This is a time to rest from all that has happened; a time to study the "gardening manual" and stay in contact with the "Master Gardener". He has a wonderful landscape design and as He prepares the soil, I must allow Him to plant me in any area of His garden He wishes. I truly want to bloom again.

You Better Watch Out

God's word is very clear concerning the treatment of widows and orphans. In Exodus He instructs that one should not afflict orphans or widows, under direct threat, or better, promise, that he that does so will be killed and his own wife and children will become widows and orphans. That is pretty strong stuff. In Zechariah, the Lord warns against oppressing the widow. The instruction to honor widows is mentioned in First Timothy.

Isn't it good to know that the Lord expects the world to treat us with kindness and respect, and not to take advantage of us? I believe that we are under a special hedge of protection that wards off dangers and that those who would oppress us will answer to the Lord. This does not give us license to take advantage of the situation, but I believe the Lord truly shelters us from harm. And for those who would dare challenge the warnings of the Lord are taking enormous risks, for I know my God means what He says.

We, as widows, can take heart that God protects and provides for us and exhorts others to do the same. I find it encouraging knowing this about my Lord; it gives me confidence to live without fear. Even the most evil of men usually have a respect for widows and orphans. I am grateful for this protective umbrella for there are enough things to consider in this new role without wondering if the "boogie-man" is going to get me. Thanks be to the God of the universe that He didn't forget the widow. I am humbled by His attention to details and challenged to be about my purpose because He has created this provision for my sisters-in-widowhood and me. This knowledge is a cloak of peace.

The Comforter

One night as I lay in bed, unable to sleep, I pulled the down comforter over my body and I felt the presence of another comforter. Jesus promised that we will be comforted and it is in that knowledge that I became subject to the following communication from the Holy Spirit:

"Jan, it has been a year since Lee became ill and died four months later. The year has been difficult for you and all who love you. Your life as you knew it stopped twelve months ago. You were both so in love with your life together that I took joy in knowing how very happy you were together and that you placed me in charge of that beautiful life.

"Lee is with me, and he is whole. He adds to the beauty of Heaven with his unique personality. You will see him again one day. Until that time, try to take comfort in the knowledge that he is happier than even you could make him. Loving him as you did should make that precious to you.

"I have seen you in your uttermost pain and despair. It is not what I want for you, but I do understand, and although it hurts me to see you so unhappy, I allow such behavior for a season.

"You tried to interpret my words to bring healing for Lee and selected carefully those scriptures that fit your heart's desire. This is very common with my children. When my perfect will for their lives seems to respond to their petitions, they declare that I have answered their prayers. However, when that perfect will does not conform to their petitions, confusion sets in and despair clouds the spirit. This is what happened with you.

"I have been pleased that for years you committed to memory many of my words, speaking them daily as circumstance would challenge the spirit. You had an arsenal of scriptures to combat the world, and it was a comfort and victory for you many times. You gave me praise for the victories and there were many; and when understanding was not forthcoming, you yielded to your faith to sustain you.

"It was a beautiful evening when you invited the deacon body and your pastor to your home to lay hands on Lee and anoint his body with oil asking for my healing. There were many angels in that room as, one by one, a loving brother-in-Christ laid his hands upon Lee's frail body. He received such a blessing from it and his faint smile was an enormous blessing to the deacons who came to serve. And then you stood quoting my promises over him, believing with all your heart that I would heal him. The Holy Spirit filled the room and filled your beloved husband as well. As you may recall, he never experienced pain again.

"Five nights before Lee came *home,* you went outside and looked up into the stars and said, 'Okay, Father, I surrender him to you. He belongs to you more than to me and I trust you with him. You can take better care of him than I. I love him so much, enough to let you have him completely because he has no life like this. You can give him more than I can.' It was the kind of perfect love I want for all my children. You were only thinking of him, not yourself.

You knew he was ready for whatever I wanted for him, you just hadn't known if *you* were ready. Lee was prepared for his homecoming; I had to wait until you were ready.

"You quoted those scriptures as if they locked me into your interpretation of them. And when things didn't go your way, you couldn't bring yourself to even read my Word. You said that it mocked you because you couldn't understand what happened. You claimed what you wanted, and when you were disappointed that your faith did not heal him, you were left confused and feeling betrayed.

"I know you did everything humanly possible to bring about the healing of your husband; no one can doubt your devotion and dedication to him. But Jan, Lee was mine before he was yours. I gave him to you to heal your broken spirit years ago, and he did. He gave you esteem and confidence in yourself through his love and belief in you. These were gifts from me given through him. That is one of the purposes I had for Lee. He brought your life joy and security you had never known. Since you gave your heart to me as a little girl, I have heard you ask many times for the kind of joy that I gave you through Lee. He did a fine job. He was a fine servant. And you were exactly what he needed as well, and he received a different healing in that he came back to the flock. At first it was because you were there, but the time came when his devotion was as sincere as any of my sheep. You were truly good for one another.

"You have sought understanding and I think by now you have accepted the fact that until you enter these gates that you will not be privileged to that. It is not because I am cruel. It is because you need me so and must cling to me for daily bread. If you could intellectually grasp what has happened, it would probably scare you. My ways are not your ways. Your favorite scripture verses have always been Proverbs 3:5–6. 'Trust in the Lord with all thine heart and lean not unto thine own understanding. In all thy ways acknowledge him and he shall direct thy paths.' You must commit yourself to this now. Trust in Me with everything you are made of and don't even try to understand this. You won't. Don't try to depend on your own understanding; that's what I meant when I said not to lean on it. It will not support you. It will not satisfy you. Just trust me with all your heart and in everything you do, acknowledge me. Know me, recognize me, see me, feel me, experience me, welcome me, notice me, trust me. And I shall truly direct every step you take. You will not go wrong in doing this. You will be on your way to where I intend you to be. I have told you that I actually send angels before you to keep you in the way and to bring you into the place which I have prepared. Jan, picture that. Picture angels, ten feet tall, with six foot swords in their hands wielding them in front of wherever I send you, clearing the way, keeping evil and wrong influences out of your path. Just trust me with all you are and you will have victory over even Lee's grave.

"I also wanted to remind you to be still and know that I am God. I mean this, Jan. Be still. Stop fretting, and all that other useless activity, trying to decide what to do. You don't have to decide what to do. The decision has been made for you. Take comfort and heart in that. Take encouragement in that. I am God; God of the universe, all powerful, almighty, all knowing, all loving. In my power I will make you who I meant you to be when I first thought of you. In my might I will provide you with the strength to be what you have wanted but never exercised the muscles to accomplish. In my knowledge I will share wisdom with you for victories; and in my love, I shall allow you all your human frailties as you continue your journey.

"You are not to fear anything, for I am your God. I will truly strengthen you and I will help you. I will do this every moment, even if you are not aware of it; I will hold your right hand and say to you, "Don't be afraid, Jan, I will help you." Jan, if I, the God of everything, in charge of the entire world, will help you, what can you possibly fear? Finances? A piece of cake. Loneliness? I will never leave you or forsake you. Purpose? I have such wonders in store for you that even your wild imagination cannot perceive. What is it that you seek? Seek me with all your heart and you will find me, and in me, you will find the abundant life. My son told you that you can have peace in Him; that in the world you will have tribulation, but to be of good cheer, He has overcome the world. Live in my son, allow Him to live in you, and no problem will overtake you, no stress will defeat you, and you will have victory over anything the world throws at you, even Lee's cancer, through my son, Jesus. Let that cheer you; that you are a child of the King. Do you realize that that makes you a Princess? Stop acting like a prisoner of life and behave like royalty. You have the authority through me to live it joyfully. Do not allow Satan to rob even one day of joy from you.

"Trust me, try me, prove me. Be ready for blessings so bountiful and numerous that you will have to pass them on because you cannot hold them all. I love you. Let's do your life in style, MY style. When you are ready, we'll begin."

I closed my eyes and felt a peace that passes all understanding and the next morning, I felt as if shackles had been removed from my spirit. The Holy Spirit had breathed on me.

Striking New Chords

I ordered a chime cabinet from a catalog and when it came, all the tiny little metal beads had escaped their package and scattered everywhere as I lifted the cabinet from the box in which it was shipped. Hundreds of little ball-bearing things scurried across the table, onto the floor, into corners, under chairs, within carpet pile and crevices at the wall. These little steel balls that were to have fallen slowly upon brass bells, chiming like tinkling raindrops, were not behaving themselves.

As I gathered each scattered ball, I knew I would never find them all and I felt as though I was searching for the pieces of my own life, trying to put Humpty-Dumpty back together again. The purpose of the balls was to make lovely little chimes. Gravity slowly releases them from a sticky substance above the bells and the tinkling is quite soothing.

As I try picking up the pieces of a life scattered by the death of a spouse, I know that some of those pieces are forever lost; but there is enough left to make the searching and gathering worth the effort. The tune will be different, but it will make a new melody. Upon setting it up, it seemed forever before even the first "raindrop" fell, but slowly the beads dropped to the brass bells and the music began. Just when I thought one would never fall again, it did and the soft resonance soothed my fretting spirit.

I believe that my scattered self will someday strike beautiful chords again. For today, I shall be content with little metal beads falling upon brass bells. Tomorrow it will be symbols and drums and cellos and violins and saxophones and all the components of a grand symphony. I am so excited; let the warm-up begin.

A Resolve

What should a widow resolve on the first New Year's she spends without her husband? It probably depends on the issues at hand. By now, I think I have handled all the legal and required paperwork to set everyone's records in order. However, his clothes still hang in his closet and his highboy is still filled with underwear. What on earth do I do with his underwear? I don't know if I can give it to someone; it seems disrespectful to use it for cleaning rags, and *I'm* not going to wear it. There are some things that don't seem to have any answers. Give me a math question, ask me who controls the universe; I can help you; but what to do with a dead man's briefs has me baffled.

Maybe it is not a resolve, but I have tried to think of things that might help me to get started and keep going as I learn how to go on without him.

I find that when I talk to myself as if my husband was talking to me, I make better sense. What would he tell me about the car, the finances, my crying? He would tell me that it's no big deal: get the oil changed, trust God to handle my needs and that it is time to stop crying. He would remind me that I am capable of handling whatever it is that has to be done. After all, I took pretty good care of him all those years. He would tell me in his no-nonsense way to do what I must and to have fun. He was so good at having fun that I wish I had paid more attention as to how it is done.

I also find that talking to myself in the person of God is helpful. I do not recommend this if one does not have a close, personal relationship with the Father, because you wouldn't know what a loving, Heavenly Father would say. But if you really know Him, and His Word, then speak to yourself through the scriptures you have memorized and loved through the years.

I recall in the first few weeks after his death, it seemed all I did was cry and stop long enough to get the strength to do it again. It takes a lot of energy to sob like that. So I decided one day I needed to get control of the situation to some degree, and I decided I would only allow myself two hours a day to cry. It was acceptable if I didn't do it that long, but that was my daily limit. After that, I had to at least accomplish one thing a day, if only respond to the kindness or gesture of generosity of a friend. I noticed that even though it was not happening fast, that I was actually managing to get things done; and my tissue bill went way down.

Before retiring for the night, I would try to think of at least one reason for getting up the next morning—something that needed my attention. It had a way of making me get up the next day. If I waited until the morning to decide what my reason for getting out of bed was, I would just roll over and ask, "What's the use?"

The course is hard. We have no idea how long it is. The obstacles of life seem more pronounced to the widow; especially if her husband took care of things like car maintenance, taxes, legal matters, etc. It used to be easy to have an idea as to how to handle a particular circumstance when you knew he would make the ultimate decision, or that at least it wasn't entirely up to you. But now, when the plumbing backs up into the tub, do you call the Roto-rooter man, septic system person, or a plumber? You are probably thinking, "No big thing." Of course it isn't, unless it happens to be New Year's Eve and no one wants to come take care of the problem. I get so tired of having to be strong. God truly will not give me more than I am capable of handling. But that does not just mean the bad stuff. He will not give me the good stuff until I am ready to handle it as well. I need to prepare for the good stuff by developing a character that responds with a grateful heart for new opportunities.

I heard the story of a widow who was almost devastated by the fact that the pier on her little tank was falling into the water and she needed a welder to come repair it. She asked, "What else, God, must I have to put up with?" The answer is that the welder who came to repair the pier is now her friend and companion for dinner and evenings out. She does not know if she will marry again, but admits she had missed the presence of a man in her life. Every trial we encounter can be turned into a lesson learned or a blessing. Maybe we could call it a "*blesson*".

I fall so short of who I want to be that it breaks my heart. I want to have victory over this mountain with grace and dignity. I want to make my husband proud of how his widow behaved herself.

So the journey is a constant search for getting over the hurdles without falling flat on our face every time. There are little miracles that happen to me and bless me every day. We are told specifically to think on these things: "Whatsoever things are true, honest, just, pure, lovely, of good report, virtue and praise." * That should keep me busy for a while.

* Philippians 4:8

Out of Amnesia

I have always been curious about those souls who, for whatever reason, develop amnesia. They forget who they are; those around them become strangers and they have no idea where they belong. Sometimes it takes years to recover from the malady and when one does, it usually happens slowly and in little nuances sprinkled over a period of time.

To a large degree, I have suffered from amnesia in the months since the death of my husband. I have forgotten so many things. I have been unsure of who I am or who I want to be. Those friends around me seemed as strangers, and I had forgotten how to relate to my closest family members; and where was home anyway? Home is more than where you hang your blouse. Home is where you live and dream and muscle-up for going out and meeting the world again and again. It is sanctuary and it is work-out room; but home changes when your marital status changes in a heartbeat, or when a heartbeat stops.

Miracles happen to the amnesiac and one day she might have a sense of belonging again. Perhaps a melody will be familiar and spark a memory. Maybe a fragrance will evoke recollections of something lost. It was the memories of all the good that made the present seem so bad. I entered a world of the past because the present was so unbearable. Maybe not technically amnesia, but as I began emerging from its grip, I realized how much of myself I had lost in that place. It was helpful for a while, but to stay there, locked away in the past would have been a far greater sickness than the worst of amnesias.

Today as I blink my eyes at the sunshine again, I begin to recall my true self; the woman my husband fell in love with and adored every day of our marriage. She was fun and sometimes crazy, spontaneous and outgoing, creative and imaginative. We both enjoyed who she was. I have almost forgotten her in these months, but she has come back to me. My husband cannot and will not, but praise God, I can, and I will return to all the things I was, and because of where I have been, I shall be even more.

I no longer suffer from amnesia. I remember how full life is. It is full of opportunities, choices, laughing babies, puppy breath, home-grown tomatoes, picnics, walks on the beach, good books, candlelight, letters from friends, summer rain showers, fireplaces, getting the giggles at the wrong time, getting the giggles at the right time, music from your teenage years, home movies of your children, sparklers, key lime pie, purple things, the word "purple" (isn't it a cute word?), huge dill pickles, wild flowers, those little sugar-chalk hearts at Valentines with words on them, John Phillip Sousa marches played really loud, opera played even louder, kittens when they dash into the next room for no particular reason, and ten thousand other joys that life is about.

I have been sitting in the balcony of my church for all these months. I have been hiding from everyone. I would arrive late and run out as soon as the last "Amen" was said. Recently I tried sitting downstairs again, but I discovered something. I no longer have the need to hide, but I enjoy sitting in the balcony. I can see better. I have a new perspective, and believe me; I need a new perspective on just about everything. I remember who I am and to whom I belong. The amnesia is gone; and although I look at the sweet memories of all I had and was, I look forward to the new memories I shall make. I never want to forget myself again.

RAIN

I recently washed my car for the first time since my husband died eleven months ago. I suppose I should feel some shame for that fact, but I just don't. I have faithfully taken care to see that the oil is changed every three thousand miles, all fluids checked and changed, etc. to keep things operating efficiently; but wash it? Who cares? Well, I confess, maybe I do. At least I am beginning to care again. But what do you think happened the very next day after washing my car? Right, *rain*.

As I think of that big green machine I drive, I think of myself. I can try to purge myself of all the emotional sludge of the last eleven months with some exercise or mind game and it may even hold me for a while, but then it starts to rain and I'm back where I started. I flip through the channels and find a program he loved (that I couldn't stand), and I think how much I wish he was here to watch the silly thing; that I would even watch it with him. *Rain.*

The early spring grass and weeds are upon me and I used to love getting out the little tractor and manicuring the field while he was out bringing home the bacon. Well, we don't really eat pork, but you get the idea. Anyway, the point is, it is now my job to bring home the whatever it is I do decide to eat; so how do I make time for mowing, sewing, gardening, earning and creating? *Rain.*

He used to brag and compliment me for creating such a lovely home for us. Now, why bother? *Rain.*

Yes, I've come a long way in eleven months; at least I hope. I haven't cried (out loud, anyway) in weeks. I've exercised some strengths, admitted some weaknesses, and tried to clean up my act; specifically my house. Just about the time I think I'm doing pretty well . . . *rain.*

Maybe I need to redefine rain. Sure it can spot the car after I wash it. Mud gets tracked in on shoes and dog feet. But here in the hill country of Texas, we're in the third year of a serious draught. So, in the scheme of things, rain is a wonderful, quenching thing; even if it gets the car a mess. The next time I experience rain that I expect will make me a mess, maybe I should think of how healing and cleansing the experience might prove to be.

My spirit could use a good soaking right now, and I shall not even complain about the water spots. "Spring showers bring the spring flowers." "There shall be showers of blessings!" Bathe me, Oh God, in your tender mercies.

A Broken Vessel

About two weeks after the death of my husband, my mother turned and accidentally knocked a cup from my hand and it shattered to the floor.

The cup was a beautiful chintz-ware cup, and I hated to lose it, but it was much more than that. It had been the last cup my husband drank from before his death. Every time I would serve him the tea I hoped would heal him, or bring him the soup I believed might cure him, it was in this beautiful cup. When it shattered to the floor, so did my already fragile spirit. I stood staring at the broken pieces wondering what to do about it. It was pretty much what I was doing with the brokenness of my life. My life had been so beautiful; holding the contents of purpose, laughter, companionship, love and so many things. Now it, too, lay shattered at my feet. What would I ever do about my life or this cup? I thought, "Father, if it be thy will, remove this cup from me."

I picked up the pieces of the cup and put them in a plastic bag. I remembered a lady I had met who made jewelry from broken china. I called her and told her about the cup. She instructed me to send it to her and she would make something beautiful out of it.

A few weeks later I received a package in the mail. Inside were heart shaped pins and a magnificent bracelet from the shards of that cup. My heart swelled at the sight of such beauty made from brokenness. I would be able to use his cup to adorn our daughters, his mother and myself. Our daughters wear their pins proudly, as does his mother. Seldom do I wear the bracelet that someone does not comment on its unique beauty. I tell them the story of where it came from and they are blessed by hearing of such a beautiful man, and I am blessed by the telling.

This has been an inspiration to me. I know that as I look upon the shattered pieces of what is left of my life since the death of my husband, I can gather up the pieces, those beautiful pieces of a life shared, and hand them over to God and that He will make something beautiful again. What used to be just a cup is now jewelry that adorns the lives of several women. God does that; He multiplies beauty into new purposes and uses we never would have imagined. He did not take the cup from me, but made it into something that could be shared.

If your cup has been broken and shattered, and no longer holds the contents of the life you loved, hand over the broken pieces to God and He will give back a life in a different but beautiful new form. He can change, increase, and multiply the purpose of your life, just as the jeweler did with the cup. Drink up, adorn yourself, wear your life proudly; for indeed, your cup runneth over.

Hurt Toe

There was a man upon a road enjoying the scenery and taking in all of life. Suddenly, seemingly from nowhere, a giant boulder came at him, crushing his toe. The pain was excruciating and he fell to the ground. He yelped with the pain, cried in agony, and wondered if he would ever walk again.

After a while, he got to his feet and attempted walking. He could hardly stand the pain but thought to seek help with his injury. Picking up a limb, he made a crude crutch to assist his movement along the way and for a while it seemed to help until he noticed the blisters forming on his hand where he gripped the crutch.

He asked one upon the road for advice to stop the pain who replied, "Take the weight off and elevate your foot". That seemed to make sense and for a while he did just that, but then discovered he would never get to his destination if he continued with such a cure.

Another passed by and the man sought more advice, for by now the throbbing kept him from thinking of little else. "You must take medication for your injury" was the reply and the man made haste to a pharmacy. The medicine helped the pain but altered his ability to think straight and soon this cure, too, fell short of what he sought.

Deciding he needed professional help, he sought a physician. The physician grimaced at the wound and declared he might have to amputate. The man left quickly and limped on his way.

Still limping from the pain, he came upon a man sitting in a make-shift booth. Over his head was a sign that said, "I can make you forget the pain you are feeling right now". The traveler was thrilled and hobbled over to the booth and said, "Can you take my pain away?" To which the other man replied, "I can make you forget the pain you are feeling right now." The man lifted his foot and showed his toe to the stranger. As he stood there steadying himself against the booth, the "healer" took out a hammer and beat the injured man's hand to a pulp. The man put all his weight on *both* feet and ran fast away.

As the man cradled his beaten hand in the other, a passerby remarked, "Oh, I see your toe is better."

Moral to Hurt Toe: The crutch didn't help; they seldom do. Stopping rarely helps, it just delays the journey. Medicine only masks the pain, and is just another crutch. Professional help might not really address the cure, only the treatment of the pain. However, if you put your mind on something else, consider how bad, even worse things could be, maybe the pain will not seem so bad. One doesn't have to have his hand demolished to forget one's toe. Consider the pain of others and know that you are not alone. See the man with no foot when your toe hurts. To the widow who aches from her despair, see the woman who never knew such joy and know there are two kinds of empty; one that has never known fullness and one that has been full to the brim and then spilled. Look at your hand and decide to touch another life with compassion and grace, or use that hand to beat yourself up for something that cannot be changed.

Boulders come against us in this life. It is how we handle our injuries that determine how well we get on.

THE PASSAGE

As I think of the past year since becoming a widow, I wince at the volcanic emotions that I have encountered. But here, at the sight of light beams at the end of this tunnel, I do not regret one thought or reaction to my pain. My emotions were real and honest and each one advanced me onward toward the light. The tunnel provided a hiding place from the world. It has been dark, but in that darkness, my soul has been given a place to rest and mend. The tunnel has been like a giant bandage around my entire persona that has enabled me to be real with my feelings and not pretend that all was well because that's what my friends and family wanted to hear. I found a place to nurse my wounds.

As I emerge this tunnel, I request indulgence as well as encouragement. I am ready to join the living, breathing world beyond the grave. It will take me a while to adjust my eyes and heart to the light, but I will adjust, and also rejoice. In my confinement I have discovered truths and simple pleasures. I realize how precious each moment truly is. I have learned to wait because healing does not occur overnight. First the wound must be cleansed. My acceptance of the grave and its impact on my future poured hydrogen peroxide into my heart. The support and love I received from my family and friends demonstrated first-aide. Somewhere along the way I learned to be still and know that God resides in tunnels, too. I could hide from the entire world, but He knows all the hiding places and meets me there. I was never alone in my passage.

After surgery, attendants hook up monitors to the patient to assess reaction to treatment. The surgery that removed my husband from my life is over. The anesthesia is wearing off, the IV is being removed and I am walking around. It is time; time to see what has been going on. I said earlier that "Life performs surgery without anesthesia and we are embarrassed by the screams." Life indeed performs radical surgery to our minds and hearts and those around us don't know how to react to the agony they see in us. They mean well but feel helpless when we cry. They try to intellectualize the pain and believe they know how one should be about reacting to surgery. If we respond authentically, we often make those around us uncomfortable.

My experiences have quickened my heart to others. I recently observed a woman who had a wedding ring hanging from a chain around her neck. Instinctively, I knew it had belonged to her husband who was deceased. I asked her how long it had been and she was pleased to have the opportunity to say his name and unload her burden for just a moment. She spoke of their love story, their home and life together and how desperately she missed him. She hugged me and thanked me for inviting her to share her feelings. How grateful I am to have known her for just ten minutes of our lives. We shall most likely never meet again this side of Heaven, but two hearts shared and cared for one another in passing, and I never want to be embarrassed by the screams again. I will encourage them to cry and weep and scream; for in screaming, new breath is taken. Try it sometime; scream as long and loudly as you can. What is the very next thing you do? Inhale. Breathe. It is taking in life in its simplest form, instinctively. It is what we do when we are born; it is what we do when we join life again.

I am not thankful for the death of my husband. I am, however, thankful for the miracles that his new life has provided me. I could name so many, but it is sufficient to say that each day has been a miracle. Each day that I rise from the bed and greet with expectation what is next is a blessing. The sun is up and so must I be.

"I waited patiently for the Lord; and He inclined to me, and heard my cry. He brought me up also out of a horrible pit, out of the miry clay, and set my foot upon a rock and established my goings." Psalm 40:1–2

THE NEED FOR SPEED

Now that I have removed the bandages of having become a widow, used the last of the medicine and put away the crutches, I am eager to leave the clinic and be about the business of living. In a conversation I had with God today, I let Him know that I am ready for something exciting. I am ready to have something to laugh about; and I am ready to consider all kinds of possibilities in my life. I hesitate to mention this for there are those who would doubt the devotion and depth of love I held for my husband. I am not responsible for the feelings of others; I do well to handle my own. I ask that you not judge me until you walk a year in my moccasins.

As I was talking to God while stomping out 3.5 miles on my treadmill, He interrupted me and told me some things. But, before you think I am getting really weird on you, I remind you that I am in the practice of talking to myself as if it were God speaking. We have had a relationship since I was nine and I know Him well enough to usually know what He would say about things, especially since I am familiar with His Word. It works for me and I usually receive some real insight in the exercise.

My Father, who art in Heaven, said to me, "Jan, you know that you are to follow me, but sometimes you try to get ahead of me. Yes, you are healing very well; but before you are ready to go very far, I suggest you get your house in order. Look around; your back porch is a wreck, your closet is a disaster, your front fence is still unpainted and it wouldn't hurt you to dust now and then. You are quite out of practice of maintaining any semblance of order. How on your earth could you maintain more responsibility than you already have? If I have something wonderful in store for you, do you really think you are prepared to experience it fully? Tidy your life; restore order to your surroundings. You could use a man in your life, his name is Mr. Clean. So, clean up your act, be the woman you are supposed to be again, and then get back to me. Be patient. I don't know how you know it is day or night looking out those dirty windows. When you restore order to your home, you will be amazed at how things fall into place in other areas. When you clean your windows, you will see more clearly what is out there. Before we move on, let's move some of the old stuff out. Why in this world are you keeping Lee's underwear? No one else is going to wear them. Wear his socks to bed if you like, use his hankies, but put his jock strap in the trash. Clean out the debris of your life."

When I finished my walk, I emptied a drawer. It's a start. I want to follow; getting ahead of myself or my Lord could set my healing back immeasurably. I just put those shorts in a bag and threw them on the back porch. Not really, but it looks like that's what I have been doing for almost a year now. I am getting ready for something wonderful, but in the doing of it, I am getting myself back and that's a pretty good relationship in itself.

SELF-IMPOSED PRISON

You are free; even if you don't know it! The door is open, and only your fear binds you. You no longer have to stay in solitary confinement. You can walk out from behind the bars of despair into a world that will cheer you on; and even if it doesn't, God will. He will cheer you in the days ahead when you are unsure what to do next. He is your parole officer; stay in close contact at all times. Follow His rules and you will not have to return to your prison again.

There is joy to be had for the taking. Step through the gate that has locked you away from life. The coldness of the grave can put you in emotional prison, but there is an escape. Remove the chains of sorrow and walk through the door to freedom. Take off the clothes of the prison mourner; put on the cloak of passion and laughter.

It has been a sentence we had to serve, but we have our papers that say it is time to leave. You are free to go.

A New Prayer

Dear Father in Heaven:

I have crossed a threshold. I have learned to accept life without the companionship of my mate. You have been faithful this year to support my heart as well as my feet when neither of them wanted to go on. I guess I thought if I could just get through the first year that everything would fall into place, and I could magically emerge this cocoon I had woven for myself. There will be no falling into place here; will there Lord? It will be a concerted effort on my part and dependence on you daily to *build* a new life. The only things that fall are usually in shambles. I do not want to live a shambled life; enough of it has come undone. You will be my remodeling contractor. You will discard what I can no longer use, and bring in new material for the new construction. I trust your expertise entirely. I shall study the plans daily and try to follow your work order.

As I took out the trash this morning, I found that an animal had torn into some of my garbage and strewn it all about. What a mess! I thought of how unpleasant garbage is in the first place, but having to pick it up again is even more undesirable. Help me learn to deal with the garbage of my life once and for all, and not dig back through it over and over. What is no longer useful, what is no longer of value to my life, what is no longer mine, I must forever relinquish.

Help me leave it alone, Father. Although my wonderful memories are not trash, digging through them constantly, rather than getting on with the present, can be a waste.

I want to do more than get *through* my days. I want to get *to* my purpose. It is time to determine what you desire doing with my life. If you were through with me, you would have taken *me* too; I know this now. So please, dear Father, as I crawl down from your lap from these past twelve months, whisper your wisdom, turn me always toward the cross, and protect me from myself as well as others who might bring me hurt. I shall return many times to your lap, but I feel there is much you want me to do and I shall therefore place these wobbly legs once more upon the ground and step out on faith. You have engraved my name in the palm of your hand. It probably happened when you were holding me so tightly with those wonderful hands. Thank you, Father; you have left your fingerprints on me as well. I hope they shall be visible to others as I go out into this new adventure to which I have been assigned. Amen.

The Last Ministering

As soon as I got the car unloaded, I changed into a chartreuse swim suit and vaulted to the beach. Taking about a dozen steps, I felt his presence stronger than ever in this last year. I immediately began speaking out loud what I felt my husband wanted me to know. The wind blew as only it does at the ocean, thankfully drowning out my words to anyone who might be passing by. They would have been *sore afraid*.

"Jan, this will be our last day together until we meet again in eternity." I responded loudly, "No, you can't leave until tomorrow. Tomorrow is the anniversary of your death. Don't they have calendars in Heaven?" Chuckling out loud, he said, "Well, as a matter of fact, we don't. One day is like a thousand; but in terms of your healing, I was allowed to accompany the Holy Spirit in this first year of your journey as a widow. Tonight I leave forever. You will have your memories of me, but you will no longer feel my presence, for it will not be there. You must be on with your life, without me, and I must be on with mine. You are unable to comprehend what that entails, but I am being pulled into the innermost part of Heaven tonight to join the saints as they worship, praise and center around the Lord of Lords. You cannot imagine the joy I sense in just knowing how soon I shall join the music of Heaven. Please don't desire my delay another day."

My voice stopped as his words did, and then he continued, "Jan, as I prepare to leave, I need to know if there is anything you want me to do for you that will assist you as you proceed. You have done very well in this year, and I am pleased for you; not only for the healing, but for the growth as well. You are unable to perceive it as yet, but it is truly there. Soon, you shall see the sprouts of growth emerge in your life. Your root system is well grounded in our Lord, and that is why you have grown even during what you thought was a dormant period. This season-less period in your life will bring many joys and much happiness to you. Dear, dear Jan, how much I loved you, and I am so pleased with your progress. If pride were permitted, I would brag about my widow. It is a different kind of pride you can not know, but just know how pleased I am to see your strength and grace."

I wonder if Heaven is anything like the beach because as touched as I was by his words, the tears dried as quickly as they appeared. Perhaps the winds of Heaven dry them as well; or maybe there is no reason even to have tear ducts there. I stopped and watched the tide roll in, wave upon wave, purging, cleansing, and roaring toward me. Then, I spoke to him, "Yes, there is something I would like for you to do. I want you to teach me how to love again." Although I knew it was his presence, somehow he was changed. There was no possessive nature to anything he said. He took no offense at my interest in loving again; rather, he seemed very pleased with the idea. It was Lee, but it was a changed Lee. He was truly my Heavenly brother, loving me purely with no selfish intent, no ownership, and no claim to my heart anymore. How humbled I felt by this perfect love. "Jan, I understand what you ask. When I see you tonight, I shall remind you of the art of loving which includes knowing how to love without boundaries. Do you understand what I mean?"

The wind picked up, the sun got hotter and I returned to the beach house and had an early afternoon snack. Then, a nap on the deck to the music of the tide, and a sunburn to remind me to take care in what I do, even in my respite. I wrote a letter to a friend; took a long soaking bath, and spent time in the kitchen preparing light fare for the eventide. With the sun behind the house, I sat in the shade upon the deck and became intoxicated by the sound and sight of the tide. I didn't know what magic it held for me, but it soothed my soul as nothing else on earth could do. I had been drawn once more to the beach we had loved. The roar reminded me of the voice of God, ever present, ever powerful. The continual motion of the tide toward me reminded me of the grace of God ever willing to come to me, even if I do not approach Him, always rolling in is His tender mercy and love for me. The tide brings so many beautiful gifts to the shore. I descended the steps and stepped onto the beach to begin my evening walk and pick up a shell or two. Then the voice spoke through my own:

"Jan, you already know the art of loving, although you need a reminder. First, of course, you must love the Lord with all your heart. From that vantage, you can usually put everything else in its proper place. You must know yourself, and love yourself. This will mean celebrating your virtues and accepting your weaknesses while you attempt to grow into the woman you were meant to be. Jan, you are stubborn, and you are strong. You will not be attracted to a weak-spirited person. Be prepared for his strength to compliment your own, albeit sometimes it may appear to irritate you. Be prepared for this because no one has ever discovered what happens when an irresistible object meets an immovable force. Don't expect him to understand you; he won't. As much as I loved you, I never did understand your moods and wild notions. But, I loved you, and all that you are.

"You love to tell and be told what is going on in your heart and the hearts of others. Not everyone shares his feelings so readily or easily. Therefore, you must, and I recall how you dislike the word *must,* be patient through moments of reserve. You do seem to jump to conclusions, and I will remind you that you should give someone a shot before shooting him down.

"I would just like to remind you of a scripture we loved and quoted often; 'love is patient.' Jan, love never changes. *You* must change. You must be patient with your own heart. I said, 'love never changes', but in one way it really does. It changes the lover. If you come to the point where you believe that you care for someone again, allow love to change you into even a better person than you already are. Let love make you unselfish. Let it make you patient. Open your Bible to I Corinthians 13:4–8 and memorize the qualities of love. Love suffereth long. If someone disappoints you in his behavior, give it some time before pulling the plug. Jan, love is kind; it is not selfish. You must not seek only your own desire. You must seek *his* pleasure, his joy, and his happiness. *That* is love. Love does not envy. Do not envy the relationships of others. Love does not vaunt, brag or boast. Leave your self-righteous shoes at the door and walk barefoot toward love allowing it to change your heart and the way you give and receive the gift of love. Love is not puffed up; watch your attitude. I never understood that part of how you loved me. Sometimes I deserved it, other times, I had no idea what I had said or done, but the point is not me, or others, it is you. How can anyone think about loving you when you are unlovely in your attitude toward him? Even if he thinks he cares, he isn't going to proclaim it to a moody woman. Love does not behave itself unseemly. It is unseemly to me how you react sometimes. Stop this. When *you* are perfect Jan, *then* you will be allowed to expect it of others. Love seeketh not her own. You want love in your own time, your own way, and your own idea of how things should be. *What* version of the Bible are you reading anyway? Love is not easily provoked. Well, you are the most easily provoked chick on the planet these days. What is wrong with you? I admit you are coming from a pretty emotional position, but give it up. Choose happiness and joy. Can you do that if you are provoked? Love thinketh no evil. Jan, don't imagine the worst when you don't know what is going on. Trust is a great thing to have between two people. Love does not rejoice in iniquity, but rejoiceth in truth. Until love gives you reason to think otherwise, believe what it tells you. Take joy in your time together and present the beautiful woman, inside and out, that you are. Get rid of whoever that witch is who sometimes comes across so crabby. I recall you tried this with me a few times and I was glad I had to take a business trip. Love beareth all things; bear this a little longer. Bear your impatient heart; bear the burden of not hearing what you want to for now, and bear with love as it finds its way to your life. You are enough to give hesitation to the bravest of hearts. Love believeth all things. Believe in love. Believe in the goodness of others. Believe in your instincts. Love hopes all things. Have a great time here, Jan, with your hopes. Hope love will respond according to your aspirations. Hope it will be drawn to your magnetism, hope it will be returned. But also, hope you answer *his* hopes. You do not want to disappoint love. You are more than that. Love endures. You endured to the end with me and how you shined. For crying out loud, Jan, you had to change my diapers! No one is asking you to do that here; just endure a little space and time.

"The best part is that Love *never* fails; and you must not fail love. Love does not fail to forgive, wait, give the benefit of the doubt, and rejoice, even when one does not get her way. Love loves. If you can do all this, then you are ready to love again. Until then, don't blame anyone else for delay; blame yourself.

"I doubt this is what you wanted me to tell you as I came to you this last time before I depart, but it is what you needed. I want you to love even better than you loved me. I want someone to love you, if it is possible, more than I did. Let the love we shared be your teacher and your guide, and never, ever fail love. I adored you, Jan, when I was your husband. Now I only adore our Lord. I am no longer yours, and you are no longer mine. Trust God; He will never fail you, because God *is* love, and love never fails. Good-bye Jan."

With these words, I felt something like an umbrella being removed from above me. It was not exactly vulnerability, but the lack of the accompaniment that I had sensed in the past year. The Holy Spirit filled my heart and mind and I gave thanks right there upon that sand and seaweed for having known such a love; such a thing in this life.

I slowly ascended the stairs and sat upon the deck until darkness fell. The night was beautiful and the stars twinkled in delight that a new saint had relinquished all attachment to earth and was truly whole again. The wind blew my hair and my spirit, and I was no longer "married, without a husband". I was no longer married, period. The year was over, and I was over the year as well. It had been quite a trip getting there, but I am glad to have survived the trip so I could experience the destination. It is lovely here in my heart again. The pain is gone; there is still a vacancy of sorts, but it does not flash at me the way a neon "vacancy" sign does. It reminds me there is room for loving again.

That night as I lay in bed, I could not feel him anymore. I would not even call his name. I would not want to tug at him from where he is. Love seeketh not her own. I want to love right. I want to honor the memory of our love with an even better display of how it performs in the lives of those it privileges to visit. I slept completely through the night. I did not awaken even once. He still gives me gifts; He always will.

Author's Note:

Christians know that Heaven is a wonderful place. We look forward to becoming residents for all eternity. I do not pretend to be able to describe its activities or comprehend its majesty. Please understand that *The Last Ministering* was written at a time when a wounded spirit was reaching to Heaven for healing. It was a balm to my soul and I pray it will be the same for you.

A New Walk

Of course, one would expect spring to feel differently than winter; Easter would not be like Christmas, but you cannot imagine the difference in the woman who ascended the stairs of this beach house today from the one here in December.

In December she hoped for a balm for her wound; she got it. In December, she isolated herself to find lost strength. She found it. Then, the sound of the sea helped to drown out her screams. Now, it is the overture for the symphony she is about to write of her life. Lee was here in December. He is not today. She has released him into the heart of Heaven. That is, after having asked of him one final favor before they were forever separated; at least until her invitation to eternity.

In that cold December visit, it was the fireplace that warmed her as she absorbed the medicinal value around her. Today, she is warmed by the hope she discovered when she removed the bandage from her wounded heart.

As Christmas represents birth, it was also the birth of the new person she would become; and as Easter represents the resurrection, it was her resurrected spirit and personality she believed at one time to have been permanently destroyed by the death of her spouse.

She has said her good-bye and it feels right. A last walk together on the beach and he was gone. It was a cleansing of spirit different than expected. She had thought that tomorrow, that anniversary date was the last day of the year of sorrow. He told her it is to be the first day of joy. Love is like that; always fresh, always finding new ways to please the beloved, and often, wonderful surprises. Tomorrow is a beginning, not an ending. A love story does not have to end because the pulse stops.

So, for whatever is out there on that beautiful horizon, this widow has no fear, only wild and wonderful expectation. What a fitting beginning, not ending, to such a beautiful love story.

Goodbye Lee, Hello Jan; nice to see you again.

The Beginning

"Thou hast turned for me my mourning into dancing: thou hast put off my sackcloth, and girded me with gladness;

To the end that my glory may sing praise to thee, and not be silent. O Lord my God, I will give thanks unto thee for ever."

Psalm 30:11–12

Epilogue

In the seven years since the death of my husband, Lee W. Reuck, I have experienced disappointments, made mistakes that I am too embarrassed to discuss, and found joy beyond measure. It has often been difficult, sometimes confusing, but no matter what, I was always profoundly aware of the presence of the Holy Spirit. In the midst of stupidity, I still felt the protection of God. In those times when I just didn't know which direction to turn, I could feel the breath of the Lord upon my soul.

I buried my beloved dog, Greta, beneath a large oak tree on my property two years after Lee's death. She was eleven years old. My children and grandchildren still speak of her with love and laughter as we remember her. How blessed we were for having been graced with such a beautiful spirit.

I was asked frequently if I thought I would ever marry again; to which I would reply, "Absolutely not." One day, right in the middle of answering that same question again, the Holy Spirit communicated to me, "Jan, don't tell me, 'no'. Leave the future to me; and My will for you. Live as fully today as you can, and I shall handle tomorrow. Again, I say, don't tell me 'no'."

The Lord brought a wonderful man into my life four years ago and we have married. I am living proof that we cannot imagine the wonders that the Lord has in store for us, especially in the midst of our agony. I wish for every woman who is called upon to traverse the course of widowhood, the joy and fullness of life that God desires giving to her. I hope that she would be willing to accept His blessings and be obedient in honoring God's will for her life. To God be the glory, great things He hath done.

"Sanctify yourselves: for tomorrow the Lord will do wonders among you."

Joshua 3:5